BUILDING A PATHWAY
FOR STUDENT
LEARNING

BUILDING A PATHWAY FOR STUDENT LEARNING

LEARNING

A How-To Guide to Course Design

*Steven K. Jones, Robert K. Noyd,
and Kenneth S. Sagendorf*

Foreword by Peter Felten

STERLING, VIRGINIA

This work was created in the performance of a Cooperative Research and Development Agreement with the Department of the Air Force. The Government of the United States has certain rights to use this work.

The opinions in this book are those of the authors and do not necessarily reflect the official positions of the U.S. Department of Defense, the U.S. Air Force, or Regis University.

Published by Stylus Publishing, LLC
22883 Quicksilver Drive
Sterling, Virginia 20166-2102

Library of Congress Cataloging-in-Publication Data
Jones, Steven Kent.
Building a pathway for student learning : a how-to guide to course design / Steven K. Jones, Robert K. Noyd, and Kenneth S. Sagendorf.
    pages cm
Includes bibliographical references and index.
ISBN 978-1-57922-891-0 (cloth : alk. paper)
ISBN 978-1-57922-892-7 (pbk. : alk. paper)
ISBN 978-1-57922-893-4 (library networkable e-edition)
ISBN 978-1-57922-894-1 (consumer e-edition)
1. Education, Higher--Curricula--United States. 2. Curriculum planning--United States. 3. Education, Higher--Aims and objectives--United States. 4. Student-centered learning. 5. College teaching--United States. I. Sagendorf, Ken, 1973- II. Title.
LB2361.5.J66 2014
378.1'990973--dc23
                                                             2014007775

13-digit ISBN: 978-1-57922-891-0 (cloth)
13-digit ISBN: 978-1-57922-892-7 (paperback)
13-digit ISBN: 978-1-57922-893-4 (library networkable e-edition)
13-digit ISBN: 978-1-57922-894-1 (consumer e-edition)

Printed in the United States of America

All first editions printed on acid-free paper
that meets the American National Standards Institute
Z39-48 Standard.

Bulk Purchases

Quantity discounts are available for use in
workshops and for staff development.
Call 1-800-232-0223

First Edition, 2014

We wish to dedicate this book to all faculty and students committed to improved learning.

Companion Website

As you will see, course design can be difficult work, and we have found that it is most effective when the process is both interactive and iterative. To support you in the process, we have created a free companion website that includes all the workboxes you will find in the text. The website not only enables you to complete each workbox but also displays a pathway for each course goal in the form of a poster. You can name and save each iteration or new design that you create to both the Cloud and your hard drive so you can retrieve your work at will or share it with colleagues.

As you complete the culminating workbox for each chapter, the text you enter will automatically fill in the relevant portion of your course poster. Where applicable, that text will also automatically fill in the corresponding column of a workbox in a subsequent chapter. This will save you time, and it will also reinforce the interrelated nature of the design process. For instance, identifying particular knowledge that students must have (in Chapter 6) leads you to identifying one or more appropriate learning experiences (in Chapter 7).

Website URL: https://styluspub.presswarehouse.com/products/buildingapathway.aspx

We also recommend using the website workboxes in connection with workshops and faculty learning communities. If you would like multiple copies of the book for use in such settings, Stylus Publishing offers discounts for quantity orders. For more information call 1-800-232-0233, or e-mail stylusmail@presswarehouse.com.

We are happy to work with you and your institutional colleagues as you develop courses that deepen and strengthen student learning.

We welcome you to contact us at buildinglearningpathways@googlegroups.com.

Steve, Bob, & Ken

Contents

PART THREE

PULLING THE ELEMENTS TOGETHER

Foreword

TEACHING IS A CLASSIC example of a "wicked problem." As conceptualized by planners and designers (e.g., Rittel & Webber, 1973; Kolko, 2012), wicked problems resist solutions because by their very nature they involve changing, incomplete, or even contradictory contexts and requirements. While wicked problems are not evil, they are devilishly hard to resolve. Standardized solutions are impossible; even if an approach seems to work in one instance, it's not likely to succeed the next. Tackling a wicked problem requires deep knowledge of the relevant fields combined with creativity, agility, persistence, and a clear sense of purpose.

Building a Pathway for Student Learning provides a practical and flexible guide to the wicked problem of teaching in higher education. As Jones, Noyd, and Sagendorf explain, faculty possess the content knowledge that is a prerequisite to teach effectively in college. That knowledge, however, is necessary but not sufficient for our work. As Jones, Noyd, and Sagendorf state, "Ultimately, our measure of teaching success is tied to the quality of what our students learn" (p. 107, this volume). What students know and are capable of doing as a result of our courses is what matters most; yet, the dynamic nature of our students, disciplines, and institutions means that a static approach to teaching is bound to fail. Our disciplinary expertise, no matter how great, will not allow us to resolve this wicked problem.

Instead, we need to supplement our disciplinary understanding with a systematic yet flexible approach to designing learning experiences for students. This book outlines an efficient and powerful process to do that. Jones, Noyd, and Sagendorf are excellent guides along the way. They have synthesized the best scholarly literature on learning and teaching; they also have practical experience gained by facilitating scores of course design retreats for diverse faculty.

Building from this solid foundation, Jones, Noyd, and Sagendorf encourage us to start our design by thinking first about our students and our learning goals. The second step is to plan for the types of work we will require students to do and the ways we will evaluate their performance. Throughout this process, Jones, Noyd, and Sagendorf prompt us to look for opportunities to align what our students do with our learning goals, to integrate discrete parts of a course into a meaningful whole, and to make learning visible so that we and our students can make evidence-informed adjustments as the course unfolds.

"Done well," Jones, Noyd, and Sagendorf remind us, "course design is a scholarly and deeply creative activity" (p. 5, this volume). Regardless of the particulars of our field, our disciplinary training prepares us well for this work. We know how to ask critical and generative questions, probe beneath the surface for significant patterns, craft meaningful theories to inform our actions, and adapt our practices to changing contexts. These are the sorts of things we as scholars do in our research, and these same capacities will serve us well as we design our courses.

Additionally, like all other scholarly activity, designing a course "is the kind of work made better through frequent interaction with, and helpful feedback from, one's peers" (p. 5, this volume). This book provides helpful guidance on how and when to share your work with colleagues. By opening our course design plans and our teaching practices to collegial review, we not only gain individual benefits from the insights gleaned from peer review but also contribute to a broader scholarly community of college and university teachers. Such collaborative effort is an essential step to successfully navigating the complexity of teaching in higher education, or any other wicked problem.

With this book as our guide, we will make progress in building pathways toward deeper student learning in all of our courses.

Peter Felten
Center for Engaged Learning
Elon University

References

Kolko, J. (2012) *Wicked problems: Problems worth solving, a handbook and a call to action.* Austin, TX: Austin Center for Design.

Rittel, H. W. J, & Webber, M. M. (1973). Dilemmas in a general theory of planning. Policy Sciences, 4, 155–69.

Acknowledgments

THIS BOOK REPRESENTS OUR best attempt to apply what we've learned about educational best practices to help faculty members design better learning-centered courses. Our thinking has been shaped by numerous authors and colleagues in the higher education community, and we are frequently reminded how fortunate we are to dedicate ourselves to improved student learning. We are especially grateful for D. Brent Morris, David Stockburger, and Rolf Enger, each of whom helped us create our course design retreat and worked closely with us to make it better. Without their wisdom, energy, and enthusiasm, the retreat wouldn't be the success that it is.

We would also like to thank the dozens of colleagues who have chosen to join us at the course design retreat each summer, producing significant work, and we are proud that we could be a part of it. Special thanks to Brandon Bernardoni and Karen Henry, participants whose work is reflected in various parts of this book.

We would also like to acknowledge the financial support of the dean's office at the United States Air Force Academy for making our annual course design retreat possible.

We're also grateful for the support and guidance provided by John von Knorring at Stylus. John enthusiastically welcomed the idea of this book when we approached him with it at a professional and organizational development conference several years ago. Since that time, he has been a staunch advocate and a careful reviewer of our work. We could not have completed this project without his belief in what we were doing and the wisdom he offered along the way. Our production editor Alexandra Hartnett has also been very helpful in guiding us throughout the final stage of production. We wish to thank her for her assistance.

Finally, we are eternally grateful to our families, all of whom have made countless sacrifices so that this book could get to print. Thanks to Kris and Emily Jones; Susan Noyd; and Amy, Peyton, and Brynn Sagendorf. Any measure of success this book enjoys is attributable to the love and support they have each provided.

PART ONE
Introduction

CHAPTER 1

Our Course Design System and Effective Ways to Use This Book

Welcome to *Building a Pathway for Student Learning: A How-To Guide to Course Design*. This book emerged from the course design retreat we have conducted since 2008 with faculty on our home campuses. We always begin the retreat with an icebreaker so that attendees can become more familiar with us and other faculty participants. Given the asynchronous nature of printed books, conducting such an icebreaker isn't possible here, so a simple welcome will have to suffice. We're excited that you've decided to join us, and we sincerely hope you and the students in your courses will benefit from the experience.

One of the driving forces behind our course design retreat, and this book, is a conundrum that exists in the higher education community. Over the past two decades, numerous books and articles have been published describing a seismic shift in our culture, from an "instruction-centered paradigm" to a newer "learning-centered paradigm"(Barr & Tagg, 1995, p. 12; see also Huba & Freed, 2000; Tagg, 2003).[1] All too often, however, the design of college courses has failed to reflect that shift. If the higher education community has experienced a seismic shift to a learning-centered paradigm, why haven't more faculty changed the way they think about their courses?

Perhaps the biggest reason that college courses have been slow to change is that many college faculty have never been shown how to apply a course design process that is *truly* focused on student learning. As graduate students, most aspiring faculty members devote their time to developing a rich body of knowledge in their disciplines and honing the skills needed to develop a successful research program. At their first job, many new faculty members look for the teaching and learning center (if there is one) on their campus and may even attend some of the faculty development brown-bag lunches or workshops. However, those sessions are likely to be focused more on specific pedagogical strategies than on issues related to course design. As you read this book, you will see that adding more pedagogical strategies to one's toolbox can be helpful, but it is not really sufficient to apply the learning-centered paradigm. The reason is that the teaching techniques one uses in a classroom are pieces of a larger system of the course, and new pedagogies are unlikely to have the desired effect if they are embedded in a course that is not well designed. A solid foundation in effective course design is absolutely essential to the successful enactment of the learning-centered paradigm, and sadly, many faculty members have never been informed about what that entails.

Lacking any additional guidance, many faculty members default to teaching their courses in the same way their mentors or advisers did before them or imitating what their colleagues do currently. That decision isn't necessarily informed by the tenets of the learning-centered paradigm, and it is almost never informed by the burgeoning research on how to help students learn. Mounting evidence suggests that our existing ways of doing business fail to lead to the kinds or depth of student learning we desire (e.g., see the work of Arum & Roksa, 2011; Bok, 2006, 2013; Keeling & Hersh, 2011).

There are several excellent books on the market that provide sound background and general strategies for designing effective learning-centered courses (e.g., Diamond, 2008; Fink, 2003; Nilson, 2010; Richlin, 2006; Wiggins & McTighe, 2005). In our experience, faculty members committed to student learning not only need knowledge about effective course design, but also need a practical step-by-step approach to guide them through the intellectually challenging work of designing a great course for their particular students. We've written this book to provide such a practical step-by-step approach.

Meeting Faculty Needs With Regard to Course Design

Our goal, then, is to assist you in designing your courses (or in revising existing courses) to reflect the best of what the learning-centered paradigm has to offer. Your success will be determined largely by the effort you put into the process, and designing effective courses will indeed require you to roll up your sleeves. You will be building a pathway for your students' learning, and that work is thought intensive, challenging, and sometimes even uncomfortable. We are committed to providing you with the support you need, and we're confident you will be successful.

While we do include at least a little theory related to effective course design, the theory associated with designing effective courses is not our emphasis here. Instead, we have placed a much greater emphasis on guiding you through the hands-on process of designing your course, mirroring the approach we have taken with our own faculty colleagues at our course design retreat. Based on the principles of backward design (Fink, 2003; Wiggins & McTighe, 2005), the retreat uses a mixture of instruction, individual work time, and facilitated learning community sessions to lead people through each element of the course design process. The culminating event at the retreat is a poster session in which faculty participants present the results of their course design work to their peers.

Over the years we have experimented with several different ways of conducting our retreat, and not surprisingly, we have found that some approaches work far better than others. Our experience shows that faculty are most successful in completing their course design work if each of the following four statements is true.

Faculty receive practical guidance pertaining to each element of the course design process. Our course design

retreat is divided into short modules that are each related to a specific element of course design. Each module begins with one of us leading a presentation or activity to help participants acquire some basic knowledge or specific skill. In this book, each chapter focuses on one module and begins with a description of the presentation or activity. We've tried to keep the opening part of each chapter relatively short to allow plenty of time and space for you to apply what you've learned to your own course design.

Faculty have adequate time and space to do their work. As we have already mentioned, designing courses is challenging work. Therefore, at our retreat we purposefully set aside a considerable amount of time for participants to work on each element of their course. As you progress through this book, we encourage you to take the time and space for yourself by completing a series of workboxes throughout the text that contain questions meant to promote targeted reflection on your part. All the workboxes are available online,[2] from where you may download them or save them to the Cloud. We urge you to pause and take the time necessary to answer the questions. By taking your time with these workboxes, we think you will find them helpful in organizing your thinking about the design of your course.

Faculty are able to interact with their peers to share ideas and receive feedback on their work. After retreat participants complete each element of the course design process, we ask them to present (and receive feedback from) a group of their peers, taking advantage of what researchers know about how people learn. Psychologists recognized years ago that people learn better when they are provided with informative feedback about their performance (e.g., Thorndike, 1922). Chickering and Gamson (1987) highlighted prompt feedback in "Seven Principles for Good Practice in Undergraduate Education," and Ken Bain (2004) has argued that the best college teachers find ways to give students plenty of opportunities to try out their ideas, receive feedback, and then use that feedback to improve their work. By building multiple feedback opportunities into our course design retreat schedule, we have simply adapted these ideas to our work with faculty.

We recognize that for many of you, setting aside time for interaction and feedback about your course design may feel uncomfortable. Many campuses do not have readily available venues for faculty to share ideas regarding course design. In fact, many faculty members seem to view teaching as an inherently private activity, not to be discussed with peers except in passing. That strikes us as unfortunate because many faculty members miss out on the social support and critical feedback that help them in so many other aspects of their professional lives. Done well, course design is a scholarly and deeply creative activity; it is the kind of work made better through frequent interaction with, and helpful feedback from, one's peers. As you work through the book, we encourage you to take advantage of opportunities to share your ideas with your colleagues, especially with those from other disciplines who can provide a fresh perspective on your work. We discuss more about how you can do that in the last section of this chapter.

Faculty's course design work culminates in a tangible product. One of the final events at our course design retreat is a conference-style poster session in which participants present the results of their work to their peers. We have found this session to be an incredibly important part of the schedule. In creating a poster, participants pull together the work they have done at the retreat into a coherent form, and presenting their work to their peers forces them to articulate the *whys* and *hows* of their course design to colleagues unfamiliar with their course. Faculty's ability to field questions and explain all aspects of their course design allows them to define their commitment to student learning. It also prepares them for the questions they may encounter when they get back to campus and begin interacting with colleagues and students.

We have built the creation of a course poster into this book as well. The end of each chapter in Part Two includes a culminating workbox that synthesizes your work in that chapter. In Chapter 9 we ask you to pull your work from the preceding chapters and present it in poster form. Alternatively, you can use the poster creation application available from https://styluspub.presswarehouse.com/products/buildingapathway.aspx. This website contains downloadable versions of each of the workboxes found in Part Two as well as the culminating workboxes at the end of each chapter. The website also includes an application, along with instructions on how to use it, that automatically fills in a course poster template based on your input. We discuss the hows and whys of creating a poster in more detail in Chapter 9.

How You Can Use This Book

Like students in our classes, readers of this book are likely to be quite diverse with their own goals, time commitments, and institutional constraints. Therefore, while we would love for you to use this book in a way that leads to the same rich interactions people experience at our course design retreat, that may not be possible. As a result, we describe three strategies for using the book. Each has its own strengths and weaknesses, and we encourage you to choose the one you think will work best for you depending on your needs. Your choice will influence how much time you invest working through the book, how you use the workboxes, and how much interaction and feedback you solicit from colleagues as you design your course.

Strategy 1. With this strategy, users read this book from cover to cover to get an overview of the course design process. This is the quickest way to get through the book, as users will spend nearly all of their time just reading the text rather than completing the workboxes online. Users of this strategy will not necessarily be interacting with colleagues as they work, so it is unlikely that this approach will lead to a deeply critical examination of their course design. Readers may wish to take this approach if their goal is to introduce themselves to the course design process, possibly committing to designing their courses at a later time. We hope that adopters of this strategy will gain some new ideas about the courses they teach and how they can improve them.

- Time commitment: Low (less than 4 hours beyond reading the text)
- Use of workboxes: Quick and intuitive. If users complete the workboxes, they will do so with minimal input from other people.
- Interactions with colleagues: None required. Work can be done individually.

Strategy 2. In this approach, people may view the book either as a workbook or as a supplement to the workboxes available online. They are likely to read the text more deeply, and when they arrive at the various workboxes, they will stop reading and spend a significant amount of time reflecting on their responses. When appropriate, they may even take the opportunity to talk with campus colleagues (i.e., faculty, staff, and administrators) to help inform their answers. Exacting this deeper level of commitment will take somewhat longer than using the first strategy, but it is also likely to yield greater insight for their courses.

- Time commitment: Moderate (about 4 to 20 hours beyond reading the text)
- Use of workboxes: Deep and reflective. Users will invest substantial time in completing the workboxes (also available at https://styluspub.presswarehouse.com/products/buildingapathway.aspx) and may solicit information from campus colleagues to help inform their responses.
- Interactions with colleagues: Modest interactions required. Users will call on campus colleagues to assist them in completing the workboxes. However, colleagues will not necessarily review or provide feedback on the users' work.

Strategy 3. This strategy will be used by those who are working with a group of campus colleagues in a series of faculty development workshops, a faculty learning community, or even as part of a locally run course design retreat. As with those using Strategy 2, these users are likely to spend significant time reflecting on each of the workboxes, and they are also likely to interview campus colleagues to help inform their answers. In addition, these users will interact with colleagues who may be working through the book at the same time. The increased collaboration will give users the opportunity to bounce ideas off other people, give and receive feedback, and explore the details of their courses at a deeper level.

Often, faculty development workshops and faculty learning communities—like those described in Strategy 3—consist of colleagues from a single academic department, college, or campus environment. Given the convenience of gathering together with close campus colleagues, that is not surprising. However, we encourage you to consider reaching out to peers with backgrounds different from your own as well, to include those who work at other institutions. In fact, at our own course design retreats, we have found that some of the most valuable interactions occur between those who come from entirely different campus environments. Peers with diverse backgrounds are able to bring fresh perspectives to one's course design work, and they

may be able to offer feedback on one's course design in a way that one's closest campus colleagues cannot. As a result, Strategy 3 may be most effective if it includes an opportunity to interact with colleagues from across traditional disciplinary and institutional boundaries.

- Time commitment: High (more than 20 hours beyond reading the text)
- Use of workboxes: Deep and reflective. Users will invest substantial time in completing the online workboxes and may solicit information from campus colleagues to help inform their answers.
- Interactions with colleagues: Substantial. Users will call upon campus colleagues to share information to assist in the completion of workboxes. Peers will also review and provide feedback on users' work.

While it isn't necessary for you to commit to one of these three strategies now, we think it is worth reflecting on how you plan to use this book before we get started. As we've mentioned, your choice will affect your responses to the workboxes in the text (which are also available online). We demonstrate this by guiding you through the following example.

Chapter 3 introduces the idea that effective course design starts with a focus on your students—who they are, their backgrounds, and so on. Workbox 3.1 asks you to consider the distinctive characteristics of students at your institution and how those characteristics may influence their learning in your course. Answering the questions in the workbox will help lay the foundation for the course design work in later chapters. Readers adopting different strategies will respond differently to this or any other workbox prompt. While not prescriptive, those differences may manifest themselves as follows.

Users of Strategy 1 will likely reflect on the distinctive characteristics of the students who attend their institutions, perhaps by thinking about how faculty members would describe their students to someone who may not already be familiar with them, and then considering how those distinctive characteristics might affect learning. These readers are not likely to interact with other people in generating their responses. In this instance, readers may simply take a few minutes to write down their assumptions about students at their institution.

WORKBOX 3.1.
Student Learning Factors 1

Part A. What is distinctive about the students at your institution?

Part B. What impact will your answers in Part A have on students learning in your course?

Users of Strategy 2 will similarly reflect on the distinctive characteristics of the students who attend their institutions and how those characteristics might affect their students' learning. However, to better inform their thinking, these users might speak with colleagues on their campuses, including students, staff from the admissions or registrar's office, and other faculty members. This will obviously take somewhat longer, but the answers are likely to be richer and more nuanced. Readers in this category would not only express their assumptions about students at their institution; they

would also allow their thinking to be informed by the expertise of others.

Users of Strategy 3 might speak with campus colleagues to help inform their responses. In addition, they might also share those responses with their faculty colleagues, allowing them to determine areas of agreement or disagreement with their peers and allowing them to revise their responses based on peer feedback. This is obviously the most time-intensive of the approaches we describe, but the high level of interaction and feedback will most closely approximate the environment we've created at our course design retreats. The additional feedback step will also lead users to the most comprehensive, clearly articulated, and well-informed responses to the workbox prompts. Ultimately, applying this approach across the entire book will yield the most effective course design.

Regardless of the strategy you choose to adopt, we look forward to leading you in the process of learning-centered course design. Before jumping into the details of our approach, we begin with Chapter 2, which outlines the principles of our course design process.

Notes

1. We use the term *learning-centered* to be consistent with the language of Barr and Tagg's (1995) seminal article. At our institutions, *learning-focused* means the same thing.
2. Workboxes can be downloaded from https://styluspub.presswarehouse.com/products/buildingapathway.aspx.

Principles of Learning-Centered Course Design

NOT LONG AGO, IT would have been difficult to find a book about how to design college courses, and given the paradigm that seemingly dominated American higher education for much of the 20th century, it is no wonder. College-level teaching has historically used what has been called an "instruction-centered paradigm" (Barr & Tagg, 1995, p. 12). In this paradigm, a college professor's primary task in the classroom is to deliver instruction, literally to profess his or her knowledge of a particular discipline to students who were expected to absorb the material.[1] In this instruction-centered paradigm, course design was relatively straightforward. All professors needed to do was to divide their disciplinary knowledge into a series of discrete class sessions and perhaps sprinkle in an exam or two to fulfill the administrative requirement of assigning grades. That was about it when it came to designing courses.

It is worth noting that all three authors attended college within this instruction-centered paradigm. We remember sitting in lecture halls as our professors provided instruction in their fields of expertise; we all furiously took notes, doing our best to make sense of the material once we left class, and we all took exams on the material several weeks or months later. For us, as it may have been for many of you, this is what it meant to be a college student. Given that we all graduated, we all felt relatively successful as well.

Because of our (generally positive) experience as students, it shouldn't be a surprise that we used that same instruction-centered paradigm in our own courses when we were beginning faculty members. We all became adept at organizing our disciplinary knowledge into distinct

class-length segments, we all developed the platform teaching skills needed to deliver the content in our classes, and we even learned how to write tests that would satisfy our institutions' requirements to assign a certain percentage of As, Bs, and Cs.[2] By most conventional measures (student ratings, department head reviews, and the like), we were again successful. Occasionally, however, we confronted the somewhat discomforting realization that students weren't consistently learning what we were trying to teach them in class. So, while we became quite competent at delivering instruction in our fields, we weren't always successful at promoting student learning. And as time has passed, we have become more and more aware of the gaps between what we teach and what our students learn.

Thankfully, we and the higher education community at large (Barr & Tagg, 1995; Huba & Freed, 2000; Jones, Sagendorf, Morris, Stockburger, & Patterson, 2009; Tagg, 2003) have learned a great deal in the past 20 years or so about what it means to be an effective college-level instructor. And while our platform skills are still necessary for our success as instructors, we've come to realize that they are not enough. Our success ultimately comes not from what we as instructors are able to do but from what our students learn as a result of taking our courses. To paraphrase Freire (1998), there is no meaningful teaching if there is no student learning.

The Cultural Shift From an Instruction-Centered Paradigm to a Learning-Centered Paradigm

Several factors have led the higher education community's shift toward an explicit focus on student learning. First, the data is abundantly clear that many students are not succeeding in the instruction-centered system that has historically dominated higher education. According to the *Chronicle of Higher Education* ("College Completion"), the 6-year graduation rate at 4-year public institutions nationwide is an appallingly low 56%. The data is even more stark for students from historically underrepresented groups, as the 6-year graduation rate is 47.8% for Hispanics and only 38.3% for African Americans. At least some of the low graduation rates can be attributed to economic causes rather than educational ones as the cost of attending college continues to push the boundaries of what many students are able to pay. However, we suspect that the ways we have historically taught college classes simply do not provide students with an adequately clear pathway to academic success.

Second, national conversations about assessment and accountability have encouraged (or, in some cases, forced) faculty and administrators to begin asking questions about what students are really learning in college, even if they do graduate. In the last decade, for instance, the secretary of education's Commission on the Future of Higher Education (the Spellings Commission) released a scathing review of higher education practices noting a "remarkable absence of accountability mechanisms to ensure that colleges succeed in educating students." (U.S. Department of Education, 2006, p. vii). Since that time, Derek Bok's (2006) *Our Underachieving Colleges*, Arum and Roksa's (2011) *Academically Adrift*, and Keeling and Hersh's (2011) *We're Losing Our Minds* have achieved popular success by pointing out areas where colleges and universities appear to be falling short. In short, the public is increasingly questioning whether students are really learning what they should be learning in college. The wolves are at the door, and telling people they should simply trust those of us in higher education appears to be no longer sufficient (Carey, 2011). The public's concerns aren't likely to go away unless, and until, college faculty respond by adopting a more intentional approach to promoting and assessing student learning in their classes.

A related concern involves national conversations about the very purpose of a college education in the first place (e.g., Association of American Colleges and Universities [AAC&U], 2007; Summers, 2012). What do we as a country want students to learn from their college experiences? What do we want to be true about people who attend and graduate from our colleges and universities that is not true of people who don't?[3] Is mastering disparate pieces of disciplinary content—what has traditionally been delivered in our classes—what we are looking for? Or is college supposed to be about something more?

The answers that are emerging in this national conversation are intriguing. Even though most college courses, including our own, have historically been organized around the content of a particular discipline, many of the things people ultimately want students to learn in college do not necessarily seem to be tied to specific disciplinary knowledge. For example, in its published set of essential learning outcomes for 21st-century students, the AAC&U (2007) stresses the importance of general-purpose "intellectual and practical skills," such as critical thinking and written communication; "personal and social responsibilities," such as intercultural competence and ethical reasoning; and "integrative and applied learning" (p. 3) that allows students to build strong connections across disciplinary boundaries. In a similar effort, the Lumina Foundation for Education's (2011) "Degree Qualifications Profile" describes five broad domains of learning that include not only "broad, integrative knowledge" and "specialized knowledge," but also "intellectual skills," "applied learning," and "civic learning" (p. 6). Accomplishing these lofty goals isn't likely to happen by accident and certainly not if college courses are designed solely to deliver disciplinary content. Instead, attaining these goals will require intentional efforts from college faculty and staff as well as a heightened awareness about the nature and quality of what students gain from their college experience.

While these national conversations have been taking place, a growing body of literature has emerged about how students actually learn new information. Educational research has made it increasingly clear that students are not empty vessels, waiting to be filled up with knowledge provided by their instructors. Instead, they appear to be active constructors, discoverers, and transformers of knowledge. As a result, learning depends less on what is done *to* the learner and more on *how the learner interprets and makes sense of what happens* (e.g., Campbell & Smith, 1997; Hake, 1998a, 1998b; Wieman, 2007). Therefore, even if we are effective at delivering large quantities of information to students, it may not necessarily lead to enduring change in them. A different approach is necessary.

Finally, we now find ourselves living in an age in which the volume of readily available knowledge is growing at an incredible rate. As a result, information that is vitally important today may possibly be obsolete even a few years from now. And if students do need information, they can obtain it within seconds by using their computers and smartphones. Therefore, while education must still be grounded in foundational knowledge, it probably doesn't need to be the singular focus of our educational efforts. This frees us up to focus on helping students make sense of the information that now envelops them. What counts as useful information versus information they can ignore? What are the connections between the disparate pieces of information in their world? How can the information be used, and used responsibly? These are the kinds of questions that are becoming increasingly important, and in fact they are essentially the same questions that AAC&U's (2007) essential learning outcomes and the Lumina Foundation's (2011) "Degree Qualifications Profile" pose (for further discussion, see Bok, 2013).

Because of the confluence of these factors, it should not be surprising that an increasing number of people have begun to question the way the higher education community has historically done business. If you haven't done so already, we encourage you to watch *A Vision of Students Today*, the viral YouTube video (with more than 4.9 million views as of this writing) created by Michael Wesch (2007) and his cultural anthropology students at Kansas State University, which makes the compelling case that the traditional instruction-driven courses of yesteryear no longer meet the needs of today's students. While you are online, we also encourage you to check out a fascinating pair of videos by Sir Kenneth Robinson (2010a, 2010b) that point out the connection between the instruction-centered paradigm and the industrial model on which it is based. Must we think of a college education as just a collection of credits, allowing students to seemingly pass through the system without any evidence of meaningful growth? Or would we be better served by changing how we do things to ensure that our students learn the kinds of enduring knowledge, skills, and responsibilities they need to be fully functional citizens in the 21st century? As you might expect, for us the answer is obvious.

The Personal Shift to Focusing on Student Learning

Just as there are good reasons for the higher education community to shift toward a more explicit focus on student learning, there are also good reasons why we as individual faculty members should make the shift as well. Educational research (Åkerlind, 2007; Kember & Gow, 1994; Trigwell & Prosser, 1996) indicates there are qualitative differences in faculty members' conceptions of teaching. Some faculty tend to adopt an instruction-centered approach, seeing teaching principally as a matter of information transfer, while others adopt a more learning-centered approach, viewing teaching as a vehicle for student learning, development, and conceptual change. Furthermore, Åkerlind (2007) suggests that the path from instruction-centered to learning-centered is a developmental one. That is, while faculty members' initial teaching concerns are likely to be focused on themselves (e.g., mastering the material to teach and how best to explain it), they can move toward a more sophisticated approach focused on the quality of student learning if the conditions are right.

Åkerlind's (2007) notion that faculty members can progress through distinct developmental stages resonates a great deal with our own personal experiences, and it has also helped us understand the thinking of faculty members we work with. Figure 2.1 represents our understanding of the developmental stages Åkerlind describes. Two parts of this image are worth noting. First, the lower stages of Åkerlind's model tend to be characteristic of the instruction-centered paradigm, focusing on the instructor's knowledge and how best to convey it. Meanwhile, the higher stages are more indicative of the learning-centered paradigm, in which the focus of the teacher switches to student learning. This suggests that while faculty may start their careers with an instruction-centered mind-set, they change their thinking toward a learning-centered paradigm as they move through the developmental stages. Second, this image also captures Åkerlind's idea that the higher stages not only build on previous ones, but also encompass them. That is, having adequate subject matter knowledge and knowing how to explain it is still necessary, even at the highest levels of Åkerlind's model. However, that knowledge and skill by themselves will not be sufficient in becoming effective at facilitating student learning.

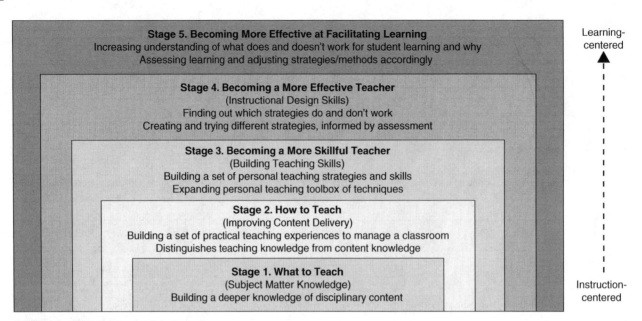

FIGURE 2.1.   Model of Teacher Development

Adapted from "Constraints on Academics' Potential for Developing as a Teacher," by G. S. Åkerlind, 2007, *Studies in Higher Education, 32*(1), 21—37. 2007.

Of course, reviewing Åkerlind's (2007) model raises the question, what kinds of experiences will help guide faculty toward a more learning-centered approach? As with other examples of conceptual change, we argue that the answer lies in a combination of challenge and support (Sanford, 1966). That is, not only do faculty need to be challenged to see that their instruction-centered approach is insufficient, but they also need to have adequate support from colleagues and mentors.

From a personal standpoint, we have all been fortunate enough to enjoy the combination of challenge and support to help us shift our focus more explicitly to student learning. While we grew up and started our careers in an instruction-centered paradigm, we've also had the pleasure to interact with wonderful colleagues (including each other) who have helped our own developmental journeys. Those interactions have challenged our preconceptions, encouraged us to see our jobs as faculty members in a fundamentally different way, and provided us with the support we've needed to thrive. For that, we are immensely thankful.

In some ways, this book reflects our attempt to pay it forward by encouraging those of you who wish to join us on the path to becoming a learning-centered college teacher. We hope to challenge you by urging you to think about the design of your courses in a way

that may be different from how you may have thought about course design in the past. Along the way, we are also determined to provide you with sufficient assistance so that you feel adequately supported in your work. Our immediate goal is for this book to help you design better courses, but we also hope it will help you accelerate your own progression up Åkerlind's (2007) developmental stages.

Building a Pathway for Student Learning: An Overview

The course design process in this book can be thought of as building a pathway for your students' learning, a trail that will lead your students from where they are now to where they need to be. In designing your course, your role is to blaze this trail and to be successful you need to determine where your students are currently, where you would like them to be at the end of the course, and the best ways to guide them from start to finish. Admittedly, building an effective pathway for your students' learning involves some fairly intensive work. However, we are confident that the payoffs you will see in the form of student learning and success will be well worth your investment in time and energy.

TABLE 2.1: Principles of Building a Pathway for Student Learning

Overarching Principles

1. Building a pathway is ultimately about promoting student learning.

2. Building a pathway will be most effective if the course design process is interactive and iterative.

Course Element Principles

3. An effective pathway for student learning must start with a focus on your students rather than with a focus on your disciplinary content.

4. Effective learning goals serve as the final destination for your pathway.

5. An aligned summative assessment will tell you how successfully your students have reached the destination you have set for them.

6. Learning proficiencies lay out the capabilities your students will need to have or acquire to successfully progress along the pathway.

7. Learning doesn't depend on what is done to your students but instead on how they interpret their experiences.

8. Effective learning experiences will help your students develop necessary learning proficiencies.

9. Formative assessment allows you and your students to monitor progress along the pathway and make necessary adjustments to improve student learning.

10. An effective pathway is clear to all.

To get started, Table 2.1 contains some principles for building a pathway, and the remainder of this chapter is dedicated to introducing each one in a bit more detail. We believe that presenting these principles up front is important because they help highlight the foundational ideas behind our approach. In addition, these principles, usually one per chapter, are highlighted throughout the remainder of the book.

Principle 1. Building a pathway is ultimately about promoting student learning. As simple as it sounds, building a pathway for student learning is ultimately about just that—promoting student learning. Consequently, our discussions of the various course design elements, as well as our discussions of pulling those elements together, reflect a commitment to improving the quality of student learning. Your success in applying this course design approach will depend on your commitment to student learning.

The explicit focus on student learning will also require you to place your students at the forefront of your course design. After all, they are the ones who will be traveling down the learning pathway you create. What knowledge and skills do the students bring to the classroom setting? What do your students need

to learn to advance to the next level of their development? What is the best way to structure the class to help them achieve that next level of development? And as their instructor, how will you know when they arrive at the final destination?

Principle 2. Building a pathway will be most effective if the course design process is interactive and iterative. Over the past 15 years, several exceptional resources have emerged to assist faculty members in designing their courses, including books by Diamond (2008), Fink (2003), and Wiggins & McTighe (2005), as well as Fink's (2005) self-directed guide to course design that is available online. All these resources contain valuable information, and we recommend them to course designers interested in improving their practice.

Having said that, we've found that faculty are most successful in designing their courses when they have the chance to try out their ideas, get feedback from their peers, and then refine their thinking. Peer interaction is an immensely important part of this process. Nothing clarifies faculty members' thinking about their courses quite like trying to explain it to someone else, particularly if that other person is not as entrenched in existing disciplinary structures.

Another component of this guiding principle is that course design is an iterative process. Our work has been strongly influenced by Bain (2004), who argues that students learn best when they have an opportunity to try something for themselves, receive critical (but supportive) feedback on their performance, and then have a chance to try again. We've found the same to be true in working with faculty members on their course designs. The best products emerge when faculty have a chance to present their ideas, receive feedback about the strengths and weaknesses of their work, and then have a chance to try again.

As you can probably tell already, the interactive, iterative process we've tried to capture in this book represents a substantial departure from other books you might read about course design. Indeed, we haven't written this book just to tell you *about* the process of course design; we've intentionally created an interactive guide that gives you the opportunity to work on your own course as you make your way through the book. In that sense, this is truly a *work*book—we want you to work on your course as you go. As you reflect and receive feedback on your work, we encourage you to revise what you've done so that the course you ultimately build gives you and your students the very best chance to be successful.

Principle 3. An effective pathway for student learning must start with a focus on your students rather than with a

FIGURE 2.2. M. C. Escher's *Sky and Water I.* Copyright 2013 by the M. C. Escher Company, The Netherlands. All rights reserved. www.mcescher.com

focus on your disciplinary content. Any fan of visual illusions is almost certainly familiar with the work of M. C. Escher, the 20th-century artist famous for creating images that challenge our perceptual systems. One of Escher's best known works is *Sky and Water I* (see Figure 2.2). In the top of the image, the black birds are clearly seen against a solid white background. In the bottom of the image, the light-colored fish are seen against a black background. This image becomes most interesting in the middle, where it is more ambiguous. As viewers look at the birds, the birds become more salient, while the fish seem to fade into the background. The opposite is true when the eyes are focused on the fish.

We include this discussion of Escher's *Sky and Water I* because it shows us that switching our perspective by placing either the birds or the fish in the foreground allows us to see the image in an entirely new way. This is directly applicable to our discussion of improving student learning. Under the instruction-centered paradigm, courses are organized according to the material to be taught in the courses. As a result, it is understandable that faculty members pay the most attention to disciplinary content, while their students tend to fade into the background. However, if we change our focus to student learning, our attention shifts to the students; after all, they are the ones doing the learning. And although disciplinary content is still in the picture, it will likely fade into the background of our awareness.

If we're really focusing on students, effective course design begins by thinking about what we call *student learning factors*, the distinctive characteristics of your students that affect what and how they learn. Building an effective course is dependent on getting to know who your students are and what backgrounds and experiences they bring to the classroom. We ask you to consider your own student learning factors in Chapter 3.

Student learning factors are distinctive characteristics of your students that will affect what and how they will learn.

Principle 4. Effective learning goals serve as the final destination for your pathway. The course design process we advocate in this book is an example of backward design (Fink, 2003; Wiggins & McTighe, 2005). As a result, one of the most important steps of the process will be to clarify your final destination—what you want your students to know, feel, and be able to do at the end of your course. After specifying these learning goals you will be in a position to work backward, thinking about the course elements that will help you and your students achieve these goals.

> Learning goals are what you want your students to know, feel, or be able to do as a result of taking your course.

Starting with the end in mind is a relatively simple idea, but it may force you to think differently than you have in the past. Indeed, our work with our own faculty colleagues reveals that articulating learning goals is one of the most challenging parts of the entire course design process. All too often faculty members tell us their course is about Topic X or will cover Topic Y, but they haven't necessarily thought about what is truly important for students to know or be able to do with respect to those topics. In Chapter 4 we provide some strategies to help make articulating your learning goals a bit easier, and we ask you to begin writing the learning goals for your course.[4]

Principle 5. An aligned summative assessment will tell you how successfully your students have reached the destination you have set for them. After establishing your learning goals, the next step in the backward design process is to create your summative assessment—the tool or set of tools you will use to determine the extent to which your students have achieved your learning goals by the end of the course. We'll ask you to think about the characteristics of your final assessment long before you think about the more specific activities, or even content, that make up your day-to-day class sessions.

> Summative assessment is the tool or set of tools you will use to determine the extent to which your students have achieved your learning goals by the end of the course. This will often take the form of an exam, a final project, or presentation.

For many classes, the summative assessment is in the form of a final exam or paper. However, Chapter 5 offers a variety of other ways to determine if your students have successfully met the learning goals for your course. The primary idea we introduce in Chapter 5 is

what Cohen (1987) calls *alignment*, which essentially means that the actions required to achieve the course learning goal should be the same as those required to succeed on the summative assessment. For instance, the goal in a psychology class may be the following: Given a pattern of human behavior, students will compare and contrast biological, psychological, and social explanations for that behavior. For the summative assessment to align with this learning goal, students need to be given a pattern of human behavior and then compare and contrast biological, psychological, and social explanations for that behavior.

That sounds easy enough. However, we invite you to think of all the classrooms you've experienced (perhaps even some of your own) in which the final assessment tapped into something different from the stated goal or goals of the course. We've experienced plenty of them, and they are inevitably associated with frustration from the students, who may feel unprepared and surprised they're being asked to do something different from what they thought, and from the faculty members, who may not understand why students don't perform as well as they would like on the final assessment. In Chapter 5, we help you create a summative assessment in a way that offers you and your students a clearer path to success.

Principle 6. Learning proficiencies lay out the capabilities your students will need to have or acquire to successfully progress along the pathway. Once you've articulated your learning goals and you've outlined your final assessment, it will be time to begin thinking more specifically about the knowledge, skills, and attitudes your students need to have in order to accomplish your learning goals. We call these *learning proficiencies* or, more simply, *proficiencies*. If your students lack a particular proficiency needed to accomplish your learning goal, then your course must help develop it.[5]

> Proficiencies are the specific knowledge, skills, and attitudes your students need to accomplish your learning goals. Students may already possess these proficiencies before arriving in your class. If not, it will be necessary to help students acquire them during your class.

To illustrate, consider the sample learning goal from the previously mentioned introductory psychology class: To successfully compare and contrast biological, psychological, and social explanations of a pattern of behavior, students must possess a rather complex suite of knowledge, skills, and attitudes. For instance, they must

- be willing to acknowledge the multiple possible causes of people's behavior,
- define and accurately explain the biological causes of the behavior in question,
- define and accurately explain the psychological causes of the behavior in question,
- define and accurately explain the social causes of the behavior in question, and
- be able to identify similarities and differences between alternative explanations of people's behavior.

By articulating these proficiencies, it instantly becomes much easier to envision what a course must include to facilitate student success. Laying out the proficiencies helps the learning pathway begin to take shape. In Chapter 6 we provide more information about proficiencies, and we help you develop the proficiencies that support your course learning goals.

Principle 7. Learning doesn't depend on what is done to your students but instead on how they interpret their experiences. In Chapter 7 we turn our attention to learning experiences, things your students will do inside and outside class to acquire the proficiencies needed for them to succeed. Note that we have framed these experiences in terms of what your students will be doing, rather than what you the instructor will be doing. This reflects our adherence to a constructivist approach to learning (Bain, 2004; National Research Council, 2000). The influential volume *How People Learn* (National Research Council, 2000) provides a particularly compelling description of this approach, which argues that students do not enter our classrooms as empty vessels waiting to be filled up with the instructor's knowledge. Instead, students actively construct their knowledge and understanding, building on what they already know and can do. As a result, what is said in a classroom may not exactly match what students learn. Any faculty member who has encountered a student who misunderstood a seemingly straightforward idea introduced in a class lecture is surely familiar with this phenomenon.

The idea that students are active constructors of their own knowledge has several important implications for effective classroom practice. For instance, instructors need to be very attentive to what students bring with them to the class, as they may hold preconceptions that are either incomplete or incorrect (National Research Council, 2000). Furthermore, students as active constructors suggests that in general students are likely to learn best when they are actively engaged with course material, rather than when they are placed in a more passive role (Astin, 1993; Biggs, 1999; Carlson & Winquist, 2011; Deslauriers, Schelew, & Wieman, 2011; Freeman, Haak, & Wenderoth, 2011; Gardiner, 1998; Hake, 1998a, 1998b; Pascarella & Terenzini, 1991; Prince, 2004; Svinicki & McKeachie, 2013; Wieman, 2007). We discuss both of these ideas in more detail in Chapter 7, which centers on selecting and crafting learning experiences that are well suited to developing the proficiencies you identify for your course.

Principle 8. Effective learning experiences will help your students develop necessary learning proficiencies. Students can have many different learning experiences inside and outside class. They can be recipients of traditional lectures or multimedia presentations or have more active experiences, such as lab exercises, discussions, debates, and roleplays. The key is to match each proficiency with one or more learning experiences that are well suited to develop it. For example, if the purpose of a particular class session is to help students accurately explain behavior in social terms, listening to a lecture on the topic may not be the most effective learning experience, at least not by itself. This proficiency may be better developed through direct observation, demonstrations, and small-group discussions. Furthermore, cognitive science research makes it clear that practice and feedback are crucial for effective learning (Ambrose, Bridges, DiPietro, Lovett, & Norman, 2010; National Research Council, 2000), so students will likely also benefit from the chance to give their own explanations of behavior in social terms and then receive feedback on their work. It is no wonder that Bain's (2004) study of the best college teachers revealed that highly effective professors give their students the opportunity to try out what they are learning, receive feedback on their efforts, and then try again.

In Chapter 7 we show you a process we use to help faculty match their proficiencies with appropriate pedagogies. We emphasize brainstorming a list of the pedagogies you are able to use in your own course as well as the advantages and disadvantages of each technique. Then your task becomes as simple as choosing the right pedagogical tools for each proficiency you have identified.

> Learning experiences are any experiences students have that help them learn the desired proficiencies, including in-class experiences (e.g., lectures, discussions, demonstrations) and out-of-class experiences (e.g., reading, exercises, service-learning).

Principle 9. Formative assessment allows you and your students to monitor progress along the pathway and make necessary adjustments to improve student learning. We view assessment as much more than an administrative requirement; it is an essential part of the teaching and learning process. The power of assessment is in revealing information about what our students are learning. We argue that an effective course design is one in which students' learning is made *visible* to themselves and to you. If students can demonstrate that they are keeping up with achieving your proficiencies, you can celebrate. If they cannot, or if their demonstration of a proficiency is lacking in some way, then changes to your original learning pathway may be necessary. For example, students may need additional learning experiences to bolster their performance.

We talk more about building appropriate assessment of your proficiencies in Chapter 8. This type of assessment, which experts in the field call *formative assessment* because it is designed to provide information used to improve the quality of student learning, will not necessarily come in the form of a graded event, such as an exam or paper. Indeed, there are numerous less formal formative assessment techniques (e.g., see Angelo & Cross, 1993) that can be built into a course design to provide information about how students are progressing toward the desired proficiencies. By monitoring students' progression in this way you can be confident that students will be able to achieve your learning goal at the end of the course.

> Formative assessment is the gathering of information about student learning in a way that can be used to improve the quality of that learning. This is the assessment performed during the course rather than at the end. It can take the form of graded events (e.g., quizzes, homework assignments) but often takes the form of tasks that do not contribute to a student's grade.

In Chapter 8 we also discuss the importance of assessing student learning frequently. We argue that more frequent updates on the quality of student learning are generally more valuable than less frequent updates (Pennebaker, Gosling, & Ferrell, 2013) for two reasons. First, more frequent assessment provides more opportunities to provide students with much-needed feedback about what they are doing well and where they need to improve. Second, more frequent assessment keeps you better informed about the status of your students' learning. This allows you to make more refined adjustments to your course, ensuring that you are able to meet your students' needs.

Principle 10. An effective learning pathway is clear to all. Once you've worked your way through all the elements of your course design—student learning factors, learning goals, summative assessment, learning proficiencies, learning experiences, and formative assessment—it is time to put all the pieces together. This is the subject of Chapter 9, and your final product is a course poster (see Figure 2.3) depicting the various elements of your course and how they work together. This poster represents the totality of your work, and it can serve as a powerful tool for displaying your learning pathway to your students and your faculty colleagues.

In Part Two we take you through the various elements of our course design process, and the work you produce in each chapter will ultimately lead to a contribution to your course poster. At the end of each chapter, we also include the relevant excerpt of a rubric we have used to evaluate the course posters of participants at our course design retreat. The complete rubric, including all the course elements, is shown in Appendix A.

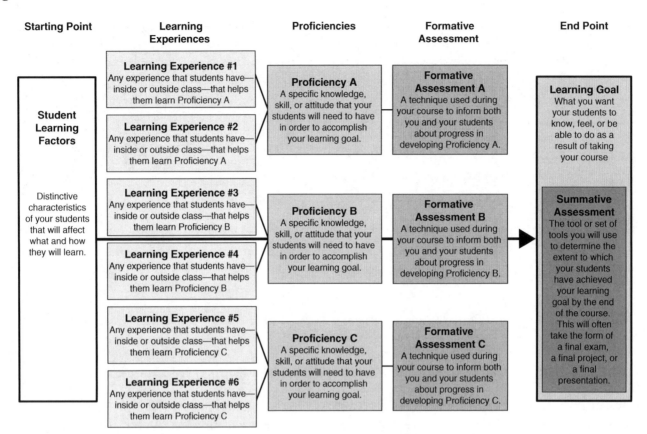

FIGURE 2.3. Overview of the Course Design Process as Shown by a Template for Your Course Poster

The poster format shown in Figure 2.3 is not the only way to display course design work. In fact, over multiple iterations of our retreat, we have tinkered with several different formats. We've settled on this one because we think it does the best job of displaying the different elements of course design and the relationships among them. In addition, we have found that this format gives course designers a good chance to demonstrate three features of their course design that we've found to be characteristic of our colleagues' most effective work: transparency, alignment, and integration.

> Transparency is the first characteristic of effective course design. A course design is transparent when it is clear to all participants, including faculty and students.

Course designs are transparent if they are clear to all participants, including faculty and students. We firmly believe that you and your students will be more successful in your course if everyone understands what the course is designed to have students accomplish and

how it facilitates student success. A successful course poster displays your course design in a way that you, your colleagues, and your students can easily understand. Your poster will need additional work if it fails to communicate the structure of your course in a sufficiently transparent way. See Figure 2.4 for the transparency dimension of our rubric for evaluating course posters.

> Alignment is the second characteristic of effective course design. A course design is aligned when all the course elements (summative assessment, proficiencies, learning experiences, and formative assessments) point students in the same direction—toward the desired learning goal.

A course is aligned when all the course elements (student learning factors, summative assessment, proficiencies, learning experiences, and formative assessments) point in the same direction—toward the desired learning goal. This is why articulating your learning goal is

	Exceptional—No improvements needed	Good—Only minor improvements needed	Needs Work—Major improvements needed
TRANSPARENCY	The course's design is **highly transparent**. The course structure can be understood with minimal additional explanation from the course designer.	The course's design is **somewhat transparent**. The course structure can be understood but only with clarification from the course designer.	The course's design is **opaque**. The course structure cannot be understood without a detailed explanation from the course designer.
A course design is transparent when it is clear to all participants, including faculty and students.	Use this space to write any comments/questions you have:		

FIGURE 2.4.   The Transparency Dimension of Our Course Poster Rubric

centrally important to an effective course design; once those goals are clearly articulated, they drive everything else that happens in your course. Your course will run much more smoothly if all the individual course elements are aligned with those goals. In contrast, you will likely encounter problems if different elements of your course design are poorly aligned.[6] The alignment portion of our poster rubric is shown in Figure 2.5.

> Integration is the third characteristic of effective course design. A course design is well integrated when the various goals of the course design work together to form a coherent whole. In other words, there are areas of clear overlap between the summative assessment, proficiencies, learning experiences, and formative assessments associated with different course goals.

A course design is well integrated when the various goals of the course design work together to form a coherent whole.[7] Initially, faculty members tend to be most successful in working through the course design process if they focus on only one learning goal at a time. That is, after articulating a single learning goal, they can work to create assessments, identify proficiencies, and outline learning experiences that are well aligned with that goal. However, many people's courses have more than just one learning goal. As a result, once we've led people through the course design process the first time, we then ask them to go back and reapply the same process for their other course learning goals. This serves as yet another reminder that the course design process is iterative.

An important element of successfully incorporating more than one learning goal into your course is ensuring that the different learning goals work together; that is, they are not completely independent of each other. To illustrate, let's return once more to the example of our introductory psychology class. One of the

	Exceptional—No improvements needed	Good—Only minor improvements needed	Needs Work—Major improvements needed
OVERALL ALIGNMENT	This is a well-aligned course. **All elements** of the course point you and your students in the same direction—toward the desired learning goal.	This is a partially aligned course. **Most elements** of the course point you and your students in the same direction—toward the desired learning goal.	This is a poorly aligned course. **Few elements** of the course point you and your students in the same direction—toward the desired learning goal.
A course design is aligned when all the course elements (summative assessment, proficiencies, learning experiences, and formative assessments) point students in the same direction—toward the desired learning goal.	Use this space to write any comments/questions you have:		

FIGURE 2.5.   The Alignment Dimension of Our Course Poster Rubric

learning goals of that course was: Given a pattern of human behavior, students will compare and contrast biological, psychological, and social explanations for that behavior.

A second goal of the psychology class may very well pertain to the students' ability to communicate in written form, perhaps as in the following: Students will write clearly and in accordance with the conventions of the American Psychological Association.

This second goal is distinct from the first one, leading to another set of proficiencies, assessments, and learning experiences. However, this goal is not completely independent of the first. For example, one could easily imagine a single summative assessment in which students would need to compare and contrast different explanations for human behavior (to satisfy the first goal) and then clearly write their ideas in accordance with the conventions of the American Psychological Association (to satisfy the second goal).

There are obvious advantages in building an integrated course in which the course goals work together. For example, when the various pieces of an integrated course fit together rather than being parts of disparate wholes, students have a clearer understanding of their overall course experience. Just as important, integrated courses push students to complete more authentic tasks such as those that professionals in a given field are likely to perform. For instance, professional psychologists aren't likely to just compare and contrast

differing explanations, nor are they likely just to write about the ideas of others. Instead, they are likely to do both. Designing a course that emphasizes accomplishing both goals is more motivating for students and also serves as better preparation for the professional world they enter upon graduation. Figure 2.6 shows the integration dimension of our course poster rubric.

Conclusion

In this chapter we set the stage for the work of course design in the next chapters. We help you design a course to focus explicitly on student learning, and we use a backward design process to do so. As a result, we ask you to begin by thinking about your students and what you would like them to know, feel, and be able to do by the end of your course. In subsequent chapters we take you through a series of exercises to help you identify the assessments, proficiencies, and learning experiences that will help you accomplish those goals.

Ultimately, you will be doing the hard work of designing your course. As you progress, we ask you to remain open to the process we lay out for you. None of what you will encounter is terribly controversial, but we ask you to think about your course in ways that may be a little different from what you might have thought otherwise. If you stick with it, we think you'll be happy with the results.

	Exceptional—No improvements needed	Good—Only minor improvements needed	Needs Work—Major improvements needed
OVERALL INTEGRATION	This is a *well-integrated* course. There are areas of clear overlap between the summative assessment, proficiencies, learning experiences, and formative assessments associated with different course goals.	This is a *partially integrated* course. There may be areas of some overlap between the summative assessment, proficiencies, learning experiences, and formative assessments associated with different course goals, but they may seem somewhat artificial or forced.	This is a *poorly integrated* course. There is no overlap between the summative assessment, proficiencies, learning experiences, and formative assessments associated with different course goals.
A course design is well integrated when the various goals of the course design work together to form a coherent whole. In other words, there are areas of clear overlap between the summative assessment, proficiencies, learning experiences, and formative assessments associated with different course goals.	Use this space to write any comments/questions you have:		

FIGURE 2.6. The Integration Dimension of Our Course Poster Rubric

More than anything, we ask you to stay committed to what matters most: improving student learning in your course. Presumably, you're reading this book because you're a college teacher or perhaps someone responsible for promoting the development of college teachers who is interested in promoting meaningful student learning. Your effectiveness is dependent, at least in part, on the design of your courses. If you stay committed to that very important goal, you will be able to design a successful pathway for student learning.

Notes

1. At its best, this was a time-efficient method of transmitting knowledge from the teacher to the student. At its worst, such a model could become "a process in which the notes of the teacher go to the notes of the student without going through the brains of either" (Tapscott, 2009).

2. Platform teaching skills are related to public speaking and presentations and include clear enunciation, varying one's tone of voice, incorporating appropriate visual aids, and so on. These skills are indeed necessary for effective teaching; however, we also argue that they are far from sufficient.

3. Thiel Foundation (2011) provides an interesting thought experiment in this regard. The Thiel Foundation is offering $100,000 grants to a handful of young people to not go to college. Instead, they will spend time working on their own to make a positive impact on society. How would those young people be different if they went to college instead? How would we want them to be different?

4. We use the term *learning goal* to refer to the desired learning in a course. Many institutions use other terminology, such as *outcomes* or *objectives*.

5. This idea is similar to one described in Nilson (2010). Instead of using the term *proficiencies* to describe the knowledge, skills, and attitudes your students need to have in order to accomplish your learning goals, she refers to them as *mediating outcomes* and *foundational outcomes*.

6. We encourage interested readers to see Fink (2003, pp. 64–66), which includes an excellent description of what happens when one or more course components fall out of alignment.

7. We use the word *integration* in a way that differs from Fink's (2003) use. He uses integration to suggest that the learning goals, learning experiences, and assessment opportunities all support each other. His use of the term is more similar to how we use the term *alignment*.

PART TWO

Elements of an Effective Pathway for Student Learning

CHAPTER 3

Student Learning Factors

The Starting Point

THE FIRST TWO CHAPTERS established the processes and principles of learning-centered course design. These included the first two overarching principles related to the focus on student learning and the iterative nature of course design. Now, it is time to begin building your pathway for student learning by examining the starting point—your students and the characteristics they bring with them to the course (see Figure 3.1). What are your students like? What previous experiences do they have? How will those experiences affect their learning in your course? By answering these sorts of questions, you will take an important first step toward designing an effective pathway for student success, one that gives all students the opportunity to succeed and reach their destination.

> Principle 3. An effective pathway for student learning must start with a focus on your students rather than with a focus on your disciplinary content.

It is no accident that Principle 3 starts the building process by focusing on your students. This chapter challenges you to think about your course in a different way. At the outset of the course design process, many faculty members focus their attention on their disciplinary content, what they are going to teach in their course. Nearly everyone who arrives at our course design retreat thinks this way, but we are purposely pushing to you think differently. Rather than

focusing on *what* you are going to teach (see Stage 1 in Figure 2.1) or even *how* you are going to teach it (see Stage 2 in Figure 2.1), we want you to focus on *who* you are going to teach. Your students will be doing the learning in your course, so focusing your attention on them will help you be more effective in facilitating their learning in your course (see Stage 5 in Figure 2.1).

Why will knowing about your students help you? First, the educational research is clear: Your students are not passive recipients of the material in your course. Instead, they see your course material through the lenses of their prior experiences, their own skills and abilities, and the mental models they already possess (National Research Council, 2000). To ignore what your students bring with them to your course would be folly.

Every course has the challenge of working with a diverse set of students who each have a unique set of characteristics. The following textbox ("Student Diversity and Learning") contains a sample of the myriad ways each student expresses his or her individuality and personal characteristics. Each has the potential to affect the learning environment and the course you design.

Second, we need to continually be reminded that it is all too easy to overlook the ways students' perspectives may be different from our own. As faculty members, we have spent years developing an extensive body of knowledge related to our discipline. Unfortunately, once we have that knowledge, it is very difficult for us to see the world from the perspective of a novice. This is a good example of what Heath and Heath (2007) call the "curse of knowledge" (p. 20), and it calls us to

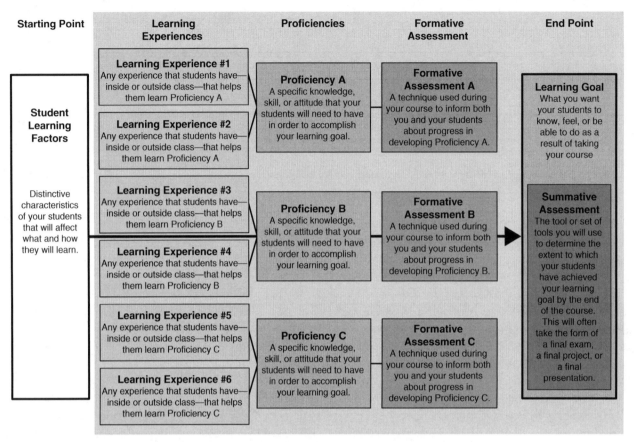

FIGURE 3.1. The Focus of This Chapter Is on Identifying Your Student Learning Factors (unshaded portion of figure)

Student Diversity and Learning

Distinctive characteristics of students may include the following:

- Past learning experiences and background
- Maturity
- Race or ethnicity
- Sexual orientation
- Disability
- Cultural background
- Socioeconomic status
- Family issues
- Employment and job-related issues
- Motivation
- Interest
- Aptitude for the subject
- Intellectual development
- Self-esteem and confidence

be doubly aware of how our students, as novices in the field, will experience the material in our courses.

In our faculty development workshops, we enjoy demonstrating the curse of knowledge by conducting an exercise created by Newton (1990) called Tappers and Listeners. In this exercise, we ask a handful of volunteers (i.e., the tappers) to use their fingers to tap out the rhythm of a familiar song of their choosing (e.g., "Star-Spangled Banner") on the surface of a table. Meanwhile, we ask the members of the audience (i.e., the listeners) to guess the name of the song based only on the rhythm they hear being tapped. Interestingly, the tappers, who know the name of the song and are almost certainly singing along in their heads while they are tapping, tend to find their task quite easy, and they are often convinced that guessing the song would be quite easy as well. Meanwhile, the listeners, who lack the tappers' inside knowledge, find this task utterly baffling. Ultimately, very few are actually able to guess the song correctly. According to Heath and Heath (2007),

The problem is that tappers have been given knowledge (the song title) that makes it impossible for them to imagine what it's like to lack that knowledge. When they're tapping, they can't imagine what it's like for the listeners to hear isolated taps rather than a song. This is the Curse of Knowledge. Once we know something, we find it hard to imagine what it was like not to know it. Our knowledge has "cursed" us. And it becomes difficult for us to share our knowledge with others, because we can't readily re-create our listeners' state of mind. (p. 20)

These two reasons—students are more than just passive recipients of information, and experts have a hard time thinking like novices do—show that effective course design depends on our ability to understand student learning factors. The distinctive characteristics of our students will affect what and how they learn. Helping students learn is not simply a matter of transferring information to the brain of the student. Instead, learning is an active, constructive process that takes place in the mind of the students, and it is affected by everything students bring with them to the class, such as their backgrounds, experiences, prior knowledge, and even their misconceptions. To build an effective learning-centered course, we must somehow figure out what those student learning factors are and how they will affect student learning in your class.

The purpose of this chapter is to assist you in identifying those student learning factors that will likely affect student learning in your course. So, we want you to name the assumptions you have about your students before your course actually begins. What you generate in this chapter will be based on your existing knowledge of your institution and information you can obtain from your campus colleagues. Once your course actually starts, it will be important for you to compare the information you report here with the students who actually enroll in your course. In addition, you will find that getting to know the individual students in your course will help you become even more effective at promoting their learning.

For now, we ask you to identify in general terms the distinctive characteristics of the students who attend your institution and then add increasingly specific information step-by-step that will ultimately describe the course-relevant knowledge, skills, and attitudes your students are likely to bring with them to your

course. At each step, which is in the form of a question, think carefully about the characteristics your students could have and, perhaps more important, the impact those characteristics will have on student learning in your class.

By working through this chapter, we anticipate that you will identify a wide variety of potentially important student learning factors. However, at the end of the chapter, we ask you to narrow your list to two or three factors you think will have the most important impact on student learning in your course. You should keep them in mind as you move forward in the course design process.

Step 1: What Is Distinctive About the Students at Your Institution?

Your institution serves a distinctive student population, which is part of what makes your institution what it is. As an example, we authors have all worked together at the U.S. Air Force Academy, which is definitely a distinctive institution. For those who don't know, the Air Force Academy is a 100% residential, undergraduate-only institution, with students from all 50 states as well as a handful from outside the United States. We have a highly selective admissions policy, and our students generally arrive on campus with outstanding academic credentials, particularly in science and math. However, our students are between the ages of 18 and 23 and still at a relatively early stage of intellectual development; therefore, they often view complex problems or issues as black or white.

As you might expect, the distinctive nature of our institution has profound effects on our students' learning and must be considered by anyone who designs a course there. For instance, because of their strong academic preparation, students in the ethics class of the Philosophy Department often have no problems with the heavy reading and writing load. However, because many of the students are in the early stages of intellectual development, it is difficult for them to wrestle with the uncertainty and gray areas that are inherent parts of that course. As a result, a significant student learning factor in that course would be students' discomfort with ambiguity, and to achieve student success, intentionally dedicating a part of the course to helping students become more comfortable in that realm would be necessary.

WORKBOX 3.1.
Student Learning Factors 1

Part A. What are distinctive characteristics of students at your institution?

Part B. What impact will your answers in Part A have on student learning in your course?

Your institution is distinctive in its own ways with its own culture, campus policies, structures, and students who choose to attend. Perhaps your institution is open admission rather than highly selective, or perhaps it serves students from a more limited geographical region. Maybe it attracts a disproportionately large number of first-generation college students or students who use English as a second language. Or perhaps most of your courses are offered online, rather than in a face-to-face format. Regardless of what makes your institution what it is, we ask you to reflect for a few moments on the distinctive characteristics of the students who

attend your institution. You may it find helpful to consider how you would introduce your campus to someone (e.g., us or other readers of this book) who may not be familiar with it. When you have your answer, write your response in Part A of Workbox 3.1.

In Part B of the workbox, we ask you to consider how the distinctive characteristics you've identified are likely to affect student learning in your course. In the case of our philosophy colleagues, the most important consideration is that while their students have good reading and writing skills, they may not be comfortable dealing with the ambiguity of ethical dilemmas.

WORKBOX 3.2.
Student Learning Factors 2

Part A. Where are your students situated in your institution?

What percentage of your students will be

First-year?	Sophomores?	Juniors?	Seniors?	Graduate students?

For what percentage of your students will your course be

Part of their academic major?	Part of a minor or other concentration?	Part of a general education requirement?

For what percentage of your students will your course be

An elective (i.e., one students choose to take) course?	A required course?

Part B. What impact will your answers in Part A have on student learning in your course?

Step 2: Where Are Your Students Situated in Your Institution?

At this point, you've identified the general characteristics of students at your institution. Of course, this doesn't necessarily tell you very much about the specific students who will be enrolled in your class. So the next step is to begin homing in on who your students will be. In Workbox 3.2, we start that process by asking you to identify the probable college year of your students (first-year, sophomore, etc.) and the role your course will have in their educational programs. We've chosen these questions because of their immediate relevance to your course. The way you design a course for first-year students, particularly those who are fresh out of high school, may need to be quite different from the way you would design a course for more experienced juniors and seniors. Similarly, the challenge of motivating your students to do their best work will be somewhat different if your course is an elective in their academic major rather than a required part of their curriculum. In short, these relatively simple student learning factors can potentially have a profound impact on how you best facilitate learning in your course.

Fortunately, it is relatively easy to find out the answers to the questions in Workbox 3.2 if you don't know them already. Our philosophy colleagues, for example, would probably say their students are juniors who are generally not majoring in philosophy but rather are taking the course as part of the general education curriculum. As a required course in the junior year, when students are already entrenched in their academic majors, student engagement and interest can potentially wane. As a result, the instructors in that department need to pay attention to student motivation. As you consider your student learning factors, we encourage you to refer to your curriculum handbook or course catalog or any curricular mappings in your department or program. You can also check with faculty colleagues in your department or your registrar's office if you require additional information to complete the workboxes.

Step 3: What Experiences Have Your Students Had or Not Had?

Now that you have begun to situate your students, it is time to name their possible specific experiences (academic or otherwise) before arriving in your course. In this step (see Workbox 3.3), we ask you to begin describing those experiences, as each one will be important in describing what your students already know or are able to do. For instance, the Air Force Academy has a large general education program. As a result, we can predict with high accuracy what courses all juniors will have taken even if they are not related to our own courses.

Even if your institution does not have such a highly structured general education program, you can still make reasoned judgments about the experiences your students have had. Again, we encourage you to consult your faculty colleagues and academic support staff to help you make these judgments accurately. Even if you do think you know the answers to these questions, we still encourage you to chat with others; it is never a bad idea to supplement what you know with the perspectives of others.

Don't forget to include nonclassroom experiences as well. On many campuses, all students participate in a freshman orientation program, a required service-learning project, or some other student life event. Be sure to include these in Workbox 3.3, as they will have an influence on how your students learn in your course.

Perhaps just as important, we also encourage you to make note of experiences your students have *not* previously had. For example, one of our course design retreat participants indicated that he wanted his students to read original journal articles in his field and synthesize them into a review paper. When we dug a bit deeper, however, it became apparent that his students had probably never had any experience reading journal articles in that field. Be sure to include any similar holes in your own students' experiences in Workbox 3.3.

Step 4: What Knowledge, Skills, and Attitudes Are Your Students Likely to Possess?

Describing your students' prior experiences is immensely helpful in identifying relevant student learning factors. However, one of the key implications of focusing on student learning is that merely having an experience is not sufficient to guarantee learning. So, just because your students may have experience reading Shakespeare's plays (or solving calculus problems, or following a certain style guide for writing), that doesn't mean they will necessarily arrive in your course with the ability to do it proficiently. We've all encountered students who had learned something in a previous course only to forget it by the time they got to us. Therefore, it is not enough to merely list the previous experiences students have had; it is also necessary to know the knowledge, skills, and attitudes they *actually possess* when your course begins.

Taking the step from student experiences to actual knowledge, skills, and attitudes may be the trickiest in identifying relevant student learning factors. For example, Ken, who has been teaching a course in biomechanics for the past 15 years or so, would like his students to be able to look at a human movement, break it down into components, and then identify which component should be manipulated to improve the movement. Based on the information in Workboxes 3.1, 3.2, and 3.3, this task would seem well within reach for students at the Air Force Academy. Biomechanics is an upper-division elective taken almost exclusively by biology majors, so

WORKBOX 3.3.
Student Learning Factors 3

Part A. What experiences have your students had or not had?

1. What relevant courses will your students have taken before arriving in yours?

2. What relevant noncourse experiences (e.g., orientation, travel, service-learning projects, etc.) will your students have had before arriving in your course?

3. In what types of learning environments are your students accustomed to working? Are they used to large classrooms? Small ones? Fieldwork? Online delivery?

4. What relevant experiences will your students *not* have had before arriving in your course; that is, what kinds of things in your course are likely to be new for them?

Part B. What impact will your answers in Part A have on student learning in your course?

WORKBOX 3.4.
Student Learning Factors 4

Part A. What knowledge, skills, and attitudes are your students likely to possess?

  1. What background knowledge will students possess on entering your course?

  2. What skills will students possess on entering your course (writing abilities, study skills, test-taking abilities, thinking skills, organizational skills, mathematical skills, laboratory skills, library skills, etc.)?

  3. What attitudes will students possess on entering your course (e.g., expectations, interests, motivation to work and meet the demands of your course, willingness to revise completed work)?

Part B. What impact will your answers in Part A have on student learning in your course?

Ken could be reasonably confident that they would be intrinsically motivated to learn the material. All Ken's students would also have had at least two semesters of course work related to the mechanics portion of his course, so one might expect that they would be well prepared to succeed with the technical aspects of the course.

What Ken didn't fully appreciate, at least at first, was the actual knowledge, skills, and attitudes of the students entering his course. Yes, they had all taken a freshman-level course in physics before entering his classroom, but for some students, it had been as much as three years before his biomechanics course. When he probed their knowledge of physics, it was apparent that students had forgotten much of what they had learned. For some students, their attitudes about physics played an even more important role. Freshman-level physics is a notoriously tough course at the Air Force Academy, and at least some of Ken's students had had an unpleasant time with it. As a result, they were somewhat turned off by the notion of revisiting that material, even in biomechanics, a context that was presumably appealing to them. In fact, some of Ken's students even confessed that they had chosen to become biology majors at least in part to avoid subjects like physics in their course of study. Only after struggling through that first semester did Ken realize the importance of knowing these particular learning factors for his course.

To help you avoid the unpleasant growing pains Ken experienced in his biomechanics course, we would like you to write down in Workbox 3.4 the knowledge, skills, and attitudes your students are likely to have when they enter your course. What knowledge will they really have? What skills will they really possess? And what attitudes (positive and negative) might they have toward your course or your course material? Answering these questions will enable you to design a course that adequately accounts for these very important student learning factors.[1]

Identifying the Most Important Student Learning Factors

In this chapter we offer several different techniques to generate potential student learning factors, beginning at the broad institutional level and working toward the more specific knowledge, skills, and attitudes possessed by the students in your class. Chances are good that if you have completed these steps, you now have a fairly extensive list of factors that could affect your students' learning. At this point, we'd like you to narrow your list to two or three factors you consider to be the most

important, and then write them down in Workbox 3.5, the culminating workbox for this chapter. These are the student learning factors you will carry forward to the subsequent stages of your course design and that will appear on your course poster (see Figure 2.3, p. 18).

How can you tell which student learning factors will be most significant in your course? There are no easy answers to this question, but we encourage you to do the following:

- Consider what you would most want a peer or trusted colleague to tell you to look out for as you prepare to teach your course. What words of wisdom would you want from your peers? What barriers or obstacles would they see as the most significant to overcome?
- If you're unsure of what your peers might say, now is a great time to ask them. Consider talking with faculty who have taught similar courses or staff who have worked with your students in the past.
- You can also speak with students who have taken similar courses at your institution. Ask them about their knowledge, skills, and attitudes when they were about to enter your course, and ask them to be completely honest.

In completing Workbox 3.5 we encourage you to evaluate your work using the student learning factors dimension of our course poster rubric (see Figure 3.2). Better yet, consider asking one of your colleagues to use the rubric to evaluate your work for you. If your entries in Workbox 3.5 need revising, now is a great time to find out.

	Exceptional—No improvements needed	Good—Only minor improvements needed	Needs Work—Major improvements needed
STUDENT LEARNING FACTORS	The student learning factors you have identified are likely to have a *high impact* on student learning. The factors that have the greatest potential to affect learning success in the course are identified and accurately described.	The student learning factors you have identified are likely to have a *moderate impact* on student learning. Be mindful of other factors that could have a greater impact on achieving the learning goals.	The student learning factors you have identified are *not likely* to have a moderate impact on student learning. There are almost certainly other factors that will have a greater impact on the success of your students.
Student learning factors are distinctive characteristics of your students that will affect what and how they will learn.	Use this space to write any comments/questions you have:		

FIGURE 3.2.   The Student Learning Factors Dimension of Our Course Poster Rubric

---

WORKBOX 3.5.
Student Learning Factors 5

Part A. The most significant student learning factors for my course are . . .

Part B. How will the student learning factors identified in Part A affect students' learning in my course?

Conclusion

Once you have determined the most significant student learning factors in your course, you have completed a critical first step in the course design process. Learning occurs in the minds of students, and what students learn from your course will be influenced by the richness of their backgrounds and prior experiences. This is vitally important because your course needs to be designed for the students you have, not the students you wish you could have. Building a clear pathway for student learning depends on your ability to identify those student learning factors that matter most.

We cannot overemphasize the importance of the work in this chapter; it will absolutely affect every other step of the course design process. If you are not convinced, think of the student learning factors you identify as the starting point of your course; they describe where your students are now, before you begin interacting with them. In Chapter 4 we ask you

to determine the desired end points of your course—what you want your students to know and be able to do by the time the course is over. Establishing where your students are now and where you would like them to be at the end of the course will put you in a position to create a pathway from start to finish that your students can successfully follow.

Note

1. Even if you are dutiful in generating your student learning factors, it may be difficult to anticipate the precise knowledge, skills, and attitudes your students will bring with them to your course. We encourage you to be diligent at this step and then plan on verifying your assumptions once your course begins. Knowledge surveys (Nuhfer & Knipp, 2003) represent one particularly useful tool to help you verify your assumptions.

CHAPTER 4

Learning Goals

Defining the Destination

THE INTRODUCTION OF STUDENT learning factors in Chapter 3 places the students in your course front and center. After all, we design our courses for our students, the learners. In this chapter, we ask you to create a set of effective learning goals, which describe what you want your students to know, feel, or be able to do as a result of taking your course. Learning goals represent the final destination in the pathway for student learning (see Figure 4.1), and your course's learning goals will guide you to make other decisions in your course's design. Therefore, specifying your learning goals is foundational work in the design process.

> Principle 4. Effective learning goals serve as the final destination for your pathway.

The following steps will help you create your course learning goals: First, we ask you to perform a thought experiment called the Dream Exercise. Second, we help you translate your dreams into a draft set of goals. Third, we provide you with some information about writing effective goals. Fourth, we have you evaluate the effectiveness of your goals on the basis of these criteria. Finally, we ask you to revise and refine these goals.

Step 1: Approaching Your Goals Through Fink's Dream Exercise

Your set of learning goals projects into the future and describes where your course will lead students.

Therefore, we would like to kick-start your futuristic thinking through a thought experiment we've borrowed from L. Dee Fink (2003) that he uses in his faculty development workshops to encourage faculty members to think about what they want their students to learn from their courses. This exercise begins with a blank piece of paper and about 10 minutes of quiet thinking time about the following scenario: Suppose you encounter a student who completed your course a year or two ago. What would you like to be true about that student that would not be true of students who didn't take your course? Put another way, what is the distinctive educational impact you would like your teaching and your course to have on your students? (See Workbox 4.1.)

Fink (2003) calls this the Dream Exercise because he wants faculty to respond as if their deepest, wildest dreams about student learning were to come true. As you pause and reflect on your dreams for student learning, try not to constrain yourself with the practical day-to-day challenges you and your students might face. If those challenges didn't exist, what kind of learning would your students achieve as a result of taking your course?

In the course design retreat, we write our participants' dreams on a whiteboard and keep them front and center throughout the remainder of the retreat. A few examples of dreams are shown in the following textbox (p. 37). During the retreat, we continually come back to participants' dreams to ensure that each person is designing a course that comes as close as possible to achieving his or her dreams for student learning.

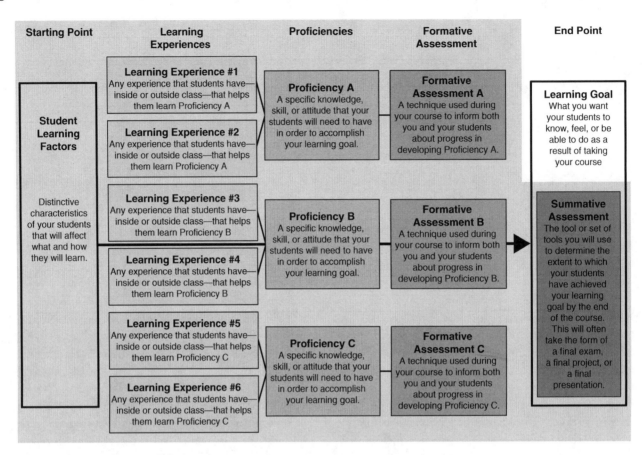

FIGURE 4.1. The Focus of This Chapter Is on Developing Your Learning Goals (unshaded portion of figure)

WORKBOX 4.1.
The Dream Exercise

In your deepest, wildest dreams, what kind of impact would you like to have on your students? That is, one or two years after course has ended, what would you like to be true about the students who have taken your course that is not true about those who haven't taken it?

Sample Responses From the Dream Exercise

- "When on a family hike, my dream is to have the student point out the various flowers and trees for her children and spouse. If the children are old enough, my former student will take them through a field guide to identify a wildflower together."
- "Think like a scientist"
- "A holistic understanding of the entire Middle East"
- "Be able to think in a target language or use language like a native"
- "Answer questions such as 'What is light?' and 'What is electricity?' in a scientific way"
- "Think at the atomic level with a molecular perspective"
- "Be excited to expand their horizons and make room to make mistakes"

Step 2: Translating Your Dreams Into Goals

By definition, your dreams for student learning are boundless and unconstrained. In this section, your task will be to translate your dreams into a set of effective learning goals through two processes—clarifying and formatting. Clarifying your dreams means making the underlying thoughts more visible and more specific. For example, suppose you dreamed that you want your students to think like a scientist. Does this mean you want your students to read and summarize scientific papers, design and conduct experiments, or collect and interpret data? Clearly, thinking like a scientist can mean a variety of things, so merely saying you want your students to think like a scientist isn't sufficiently clear to guide your course decisions.

Use Workbox 4.2 to write down what your dreams for student learning mean, keeping in mind the student learning factors for the course you are designing. For example, thinking like a scientist may be different for first-year versus senior students.

Another process takes your clarified dreams and puts them into the proper format. So let's first look at the general format of learning goals. Keep in mind

---

WORKBOX 4.2.
Dream Clarification

Clarify what you mean by your dream:

that a learning goal is a statement of what you want your students to know, feel, or be able to do as a result of taking your course.

Effective goals are visible and focus on student performance; therefore, your statement starts with the phrase "Students will be able to . . ." and continues with an action verb that says what students will do to demonstrate their learning, such as *analyze, predict, design,* or *explain.* The verb is followed by either the object of the action (what they act on) or the learning product.

Bloom's (1956) taxonomy (see also Anderson & Krathwohl, 2001) is an excellent tool for selecting the appropriate action verb for your goal. Figure 4.2 contains verbs associated with the cognitive domain of Bloom's taxonomy. Verbs associated with the affective (emotional) and psychomotor domains of learning are listed in Appendix B.

General Format for Learning Goal

Students will be able to [action verb followed by object or product of action verb].

Let's examine a specific learning goal from a biomechanics course.

Students will be able to identify the functional anatomy.

The intended goal of instruction here is to have students identify the functional anatomy, which is under the category of comprehension in the cognitive domain of Bloom's taxonomy, shown in Figure 4.2. In our example, the learning product refers to the object of their action, or what they identify: the functional anatomy. The action verb and the learning product is the format of a learning goal.

Many retreat participants find it useful to begin their goals statement with a scenario, situation, or condition for students to explain, analyze, or predict. A learning scenario is a real-life situation professionals often face in their practice (Errington, 2003). Scenarios are commonly used to motivate and help students connect and integrate their knowledge with professional practice. These types of goal statements often

Knowledge	Comprehension	Application	Analysis	Synthesis	Evaluation
Categorize	Restate	Apply	Analyze	Arrange	Appraise
Define	Describe	Demonstrate	Appraise	Assemble	Arrange
Describe	Discuss	Diagram	Break down	Categorize	Assess
Identify	Distinguish	Discover	Calculate	Collect	Choose
Label	Explain	Modify	Categorize	Combine	Compare
List	Generalize	Interpret	Compare	Compose	Conclude
Match	Identify	Illustrate	Contrast	Construct	Critique
Name	Illustrate	Operate	Criticize	Create	Criticize
Outline	Locate	Predict	Debate	Design	Explain
Recall	Paraphrase	Produce	Diagram	Devise	Diagnose
Repeat	Recognize	Show	Distinguish	Explain	Estimate
Select	Summarize	Sketch	Examine	Formulate	Evaluate
State	Tell	Use	Relate	Invent	Judge
	Translate		Separate	Manage	Justify
			Solve	Organize	Measure
			Test	Plan	Rate
				Prepare	Recommend
				Propose	Revise
				Rearrange	Score
				Reconstruct	Select
					Support
					Value

FIGURE 4.2.   **The Cognitive Domain of Bloom's (1956) Taxonomy of Educational Objectives**

begin with "Given a . . ." preceding the action verb. The biomechanics example in the following textbox starts with a condition, "Given a human movement," which is followed by a goal—what students do with their observation of a body movement. From this goal it is clear the students will be learning about a variety of human body movements in this course.

> ### Sample Learning Goal for Biomechanics
>
> Given a human movement, students will be able to identify the functional anatomy.

Other examples using this format are "Given a couple's financial situation and goals, students will be able to produce specific financial recommendations" or "Given a company's financial statement, students will be able to evaluate the financial health of the company." You can use a variety of situations from simple to complex throughout the course, which is a major benefit of using this scenario approach.

Another twist on the format is using terms in parentheses to elucidate and clarify the meaning of *functional anatomy*. This is another way to help your students and others clearly understand your goal. You may want to consider using scenarios and parenthetical terms in developing your goals.

> ### Sample Learning Goal for Biomechanics
>
> Given a human movement, students will be able to identify the functional anatomy (muscles, tendons, ligaments) involved.

While this single learning goal is an important part of a biomechanics course, it probably is not sufficient to fulfill the instructor's dreams of student learning. The complete set of learning goals for this course adheres to the basic format; the goals focus on what students do in a particular situation (given a body movement), and the text in parentheses allows the instructor to clarify unfamiliar terms. Collectively, the goals provide a foundation for designing a course that fulfills the instructor's dreams.

In Workbox 4.3 make your first attempt at writing a set of learning goals for your course. As a general

> ### Learning Goals for Biomechanics
>
> Given a human movement, students will be able to:
>
> 1. Identify the functional anatomy (muscles, tendons, ligaments)
> 2. Predict the forces acting on the joints and the ways they change during movement
> 3. Evaluate performance on the basis of biomechanical factors (e.g., forces, velocities, angles, etc.)
> 4. Explain the movement using the language and principles of biomechanics

rule, courses have a set of learning goals that include between three to five goal statements. If there are fewer than three, the goals are likely to be so general they won't be very informative. On the other hand, if there are more than five, the goals are likely to lack the generality needed to span the entire course and would thus be much closer to what we call *proficiencies*, which we discuss in Chapter 6.

Step 3: Refining Your Goals

Now that you have clarified and formatted your dream into a set of goals, it is time to refine them so they are really powerful and effective. In fact, this is some of the most rewarding work we do at our course design retreat. In this step you will evaluate your goals against five criteria of effectiveness.[1] An effective learning goal clearly communicates your intent for student learning and therefore meets the five criteria listed in the next textbox, which you will use to evaluate your goals.

> ### Characteristics of Effective Goals
>
> An effective learning goal:
>
> 1. Is clear and understandable to all
> 2. Focuses on student performance
> 3. Requires a high level of thinking that is developmentally appropriate
> 4. Connects components of the course
> 5. Is worthwhile and significant

WORKBOX 4.3.
Your Course Learning Goals

Write down a set of your learning goals in the proper format.

- Students will be able to [action verb followed by object or learning product]

Or

- Given [scenario, situation, etc.] students will be able to [action verb followed by object or learning product].

In the following sections, for each criterion, we provide a poor example, a commentary on why it is ineffective, and the ways it can be improved. In most cases, we explain why the better example is an improved version of the poor one.

Characteristic 1: An Effective Learning Goal Is Clear and Understandable

Clarity is the gateway characteristic; without clarity the goal doesn't function and loses its power. The goal must be clear to students and colleagues so that everyone has a clear picture of your intended learning outcome. Clear goals are generally phrased in fairly simple terms rather than in a complex, dense set of terms. Clarity is especially challenging when you have to communicate to people outside your discipline;

therefore, it is important to use few technical terms and avoid acronyms and jargon. This is where the use of additional or parenthetical language can be helpful to clarify words that may be unfamiliar to people outside your discipline.

Course: Upper-level English course, Literary Criticism

Poor example: Students will be able to understand the various critical applications to literary texts and succeed in practicing selected approaches.

Commentary: The verb understand *can be interpreted many different ways. The phrases* various critical applications *and* practicing selected approaches *are not clear and need to be revised in easy-to-understand language. A common pitfall is crafting a goal that is clear to the instructor but not to students or others outside the subject* area. *In the following improved goal we use additional language to further clarify the meaning of* critique.

Better example: Students will be able to critique a literary work by breaking it down into its component parts, interpreting its meaning, and weighing its strengths and weaknesses.

Commentary: This language shows students what the term critique *means in simple language, giving students a clearer picture of what they will be expected to do in this course.*

Characteristic 2: An Effective Learning Goal Focuses on Student Performance

The purpose of goals is to focus on student learning; therefore, course goals describe what students should be able to do at the end of the course. The phrase *be able to do* may mean doing something mentally, physically, or emotionally. Bloom's (1956) taxonomy of the cognitive domain (see also Anderson & Krathwohl, 2001) links particular action verbs to various levels of thinking (see Figure 4.2; note that as one moves from left to right in this figure, there is a step up in the complexity of thinking required by students). However, besides the cognitive domain, there are also other important kinds of learning that faculty care about as well. As a result, Bloom's taxonomy also includes two other learning domains: physical skills (psychomotor; see Simpson, 1972) and feelings (affective; see Krathwohl, Bloom, & Masia, 1964). For your convenience, we include figures of these two additional learning domains in Appendix B. It is important to identify all the ways that students will perform differently as a result of taking your course; this will focus your attention on the totality of your students' learning.

Course: Upper-level psychology course, Theories of Personality

Poor example: My goal is to provide you with an opportunity to learn and apply personality of psychology knowledge and processes to your personal and professional development.

Commentary: This goal is written from the instructor's perspective (provide you with an opportunity) *rather than as something he or she wants the students to do. The student-focused piece of this statement is unclear and vague* (to learn and apply psychology knowledge) *because it doesn't specify what students will be able to do* (learn?) *that is visible and measurable.*

Better example: Students will be able to identify elements of their own personality (motives, emotions, thoughts) and describe the role these elements play in their personal and professional development.

Commentary: The better example improves the goal in two ways: It states the learning goal in terms of what students will do rather than what the instructor will do, and it clearly shows students what they will be doing in the course (looking at various aspects of their own personality and and how each part will influence their future development).

Characteristic 3: An Effective Learning Goal Requires High Levels of Developmentally Appropriate Thinking

Course learning goals are generally written with action verbs at the higher levels of thinking, shown in the top four steps in Figure 4.2. This does not mean that fundamental knowledge or skills are unimportant. Indeed, Bloom's (1956) taxonomy is hierarchical, and high-level goals are supported by lower-level proficiencies, which we explore in more detail in Chapter 6. Many introductory courses focus solely on low-level learning, assuming that students will perform high levels of thinking on their own or in subsequent courses. Why reserve high-level goals for upper-level courses? This is analogous to asking musicians in introductory performing arts courses to practice only individual notes and scales without ever putting them together in songs. To become a good musician, one must play musical notes in the context of how they're used, just as low-level knowledge is most meaningful when it is learned in the context of how it is used. Think about and write goals that ask students to apply, interpret, analyze, synthesize, evaluate, create, or design. Some verbs, such as *explain* or *identify,* can represent lower or higher levels of thinking depending on the context, depth, and complexity of the learning task. It is important to choose your action verbs carefully because they will ultimately determine the kinds of learning experiences and assessments you will use in your class.

Goals that are developmentally appropriate directly address student learning factors you identified in Chapter 3. Students vary in terms of their confidence, life experiences, and backgrounds, so this is an especially challenging criterion for someone other than you to evaluate. There is no single right answer to whether your goal is developmentally appropriate for some or most of your students. Students will rise to high expectations; however, if goals are too challenging, students will become frustrated at their inability to accomplish them. If goals are too easy, they become bored. The challenge is to create course goals that are challenging yet achievable for the students in your class.

Course: Upper-level management course, Financial Accounting

Poor example: Students will be able to list and describe factors that drive the performance of a company.

Commentary: The action verbs list *and* describe *are at the lower levels of Bloom's (1956) taxonomy (see Figure 4.2) and focus on the skill of remembering, rather than the higher levels of synthesis, application, and analysis. While it is important to know this information, it can be assimilated into a course goal that demands a higher level of thinking from students.*

Better example: Given a financial report, students will be able to evaluate current performance of a company for a given external stakeholder (e.g., investor, customers, creditors, suppliers).

Commentary: By using the action verb evaluate, *the goal signals to students that they will take the role of external stakeholder of a company. They will learn financial terms and information, understand the meaning of that information, and pull together and apply the information so they will be able predict the future performance of the company. It is an example of an effective scenario-based goal because it is clear, requires high-level thinking, and guides the course design process.*

Characteristic 4: An Effective Learning Goal Connects Components of the Course

This criterion addresses the integrative quality of course learning goals. An effective learning goal connects and weaves together the many parts of the course. It's easy to fall into the trap of creating goals that are a collection of smaller units of study, as shown in the following example.

Course: Introductory philosophy course, Comparative Religion

Poor example: Students will be able to explain the major beliefs and divisions of the following religious traditions: Hinduism, Buddhism, Jainism, Sikhism, Zoroastrianism, Judaism, and Christianity.

Commentary: We imagine this course tackles the beliefs and divisions of each of the religious traditions as separate units of study. However, course designers' dreams are usually driven by helping students make connections across course material rather than merely giving them collections of that material. This learning goal reflects a collection of course material, which falls short of the more connective dream.

Better example: Students will be able to compare and contrast the major beliefs and divisions of the following religious traditions: Hinduism, Buddhism, Jainism, Sikhism, Zoroastrianism, Judaism, and Christianity.

Commentary: This is a more connective goal because it is aligned with the course title (Comparative Religion) and asks students to examine their knowledge and look for similarities and differences among the different religions. This example shows the importance of the action verb. Changing the verb explain *to compare* results in a different learning goal altogether.*

Characteristic 5: An Effective Learning Goal Is Worthwhile and Significant

Your dream most likely has your students accomplishing worthwhile and significant learning that lasts. An effective strategy many instructors use to meet this criterion involves authentic tasks in which students face challenges similar to those faced by professionals in the field. Students find authentic tasks highly motivating, and they easily see the relevance of completing them (Yair, 2000). As a result, they are more likely to perform their best work. Obviously, we wouldn't expect the work of beginning students to be as good as the work of professionals; nonetheless, authentic tasks usually elicit the students' very best efforts. Ask yourself what professionals in your field do and how you could incorporate elements of those tasks into your course.

Course: Introductory aeronautical engineering course for nonmajors, Fundamentals of Aeronautics

Poor example: Perform calculations on the basis of existing wing designs.

Commentary: On the surface, it may seem sensible to expect students in an introductory course to perform calculations on the basis of existing wing designs. However, merely performing calculations will not elicit students' best efforts, particularly if those students are not aspiring aeronautical engineering majors. Students need to understand why those calculations are needed, so providing a meaningful context (from the students' perspective) for their work is important.

Better example: Given a set of proposed aircraft specifications (frame, power, purpose), students will produce an innovative wing design.

Commentary: This goal places students in the role of aeronautical engineer—a more meaningful and motivating context. Here, they use calculations to design the wings of an aircraft. This is what professionals do in this field. Engineering courses are natural areas where students can perform tasks similar to those of professionals, such as design and build bridges, roads, electrical circuitry, or engines.

Step 4: Evaluating the Effectiveness of Your Goals

Throughout the design process we ask you to stop and consider a few questions about the work you have accomplished. Now examine your set of goals from Workbox 4.3 by asking yourself the following: If students accomplish the goals you have written, will they also accomplish your dream? If you answer *no* to this question, your goals need to be revised. How well do your goals meet the criteria for the following:

- clarity—are your verbs clear, or do they need further elaboration and explanation?
- a focus on student performance—can you see what students will actually do to meet this goal?
- developmentally appropriate high levels of thinking—do your goals challenge students to mentally grow and develop, and can students enrolled in the class actually accomplish these goals?
- connection among all aspects of the course—does each of your goals bring together underlying proficiencies, and are your goals the terminal behavior that connects a set of proficiencies and learning experiences along the learning pathway?
- worthwhileness and significance—is this goal worth spending your energy, resources,

and time on, are you willing to allocate the necessary class time to help students achieve the goal, and what will you do to motivate students to work hard to accomplish these goals?

Step 5: Revising and Refining Your Goals: Check for Common Pitfalls

Up to this point, you have drafted a set of your course learning goals and evaluated them for their effectiveness. They are just about ready to be presented to your colleagues, peers, or friends for feedback. However, before taking that step, let us review a few common pitfalls we have encountered in working with our own faculty colleagues so you can be sure to avoid them as you move forward.

Pitfall 1: Vague Terminology

Using verb phrases that are vague, unfocused, and open to many different interpretations, such as *to know*, *to understand*, *to demonstrate knowledge of*, and *to discuss*, is the first pitfall. It is very tempting to use these verbs when writing a learning goal because they often lie at the heart of what we want students to achieve; we value understanding experiences, concepts, objects, processes, people, and events in our disciplines. We want students to have a rich body of knowledge they can use and discuss with us in service to higher levels of thinking. However, we agree with Gardner (1999) that these words are not clear because they are too complex, too broad, and fail to give the student a clear, actionable outcome. These verbs keep students guessing about how to study the material and prompt the questions, "What do you mean by that?" and "Is that going to be on the test?" This pitfall is a direct result of not heeding the first gateway criterion of effective goals—clarity.

Often, faculty use verbs such as *understand* when they are not really sure or have a vague notion of what understanding means or looks like. What you want students to understand can serve as a starting point to think about what you want students to do to demonstrate their learning. The task is to begin analyzing your thinking about the word. White and Grunstone (1992) seek to clarify the meaning of *understanding* with the following questions: Do you mean to understand a concept, a single piece of knowledge, or a whole discipline? Do you mean understanding people, situations, or a communication? How deeply do you expect students to understand—on a fairly superficial level or a highly connective, deeper level? How many different elements do you expect your students to connect? How refined and subtly do you expect them to connect the elements? What does it mean to understand or grasp an idea? Providing clear answers to these questions will move you along the process of drafting and writing your course goals.

Pitfall 2: Too Much Focus on Content

This pitfall involves focusing too much on course on content rather than on what students do with the content. We professors tend to be strongly wedded to the content; our professional identity centers on it. If we are not careful, our identification with content can become a great weakness as we formulate our learning goals. To be clear, guiding students to build a strong foundation of knowledge and conceptual understanding is important to every college course. Falling into this pitfall is ignoring the third criterion of effectiveness—high levels of thinking. Again, it is important to emphasize that content is most meaningful when it is learned in the context of how it is used. To reach higher levels of thinking, students must master and connect specific concepts; they must learn the language of your discipline so they are able to communicate and build strong mental models. We are not saying that content is unimportant, rather we urge you to focus on the student and what he or she does with the content rather than on the content itself. Falling into this pitfall may leave you with a course that is more about teaching your disciplinary content rather than teaching students to accomplish learning goals.

Pitfall 3: Confusing Goals and Experiences

Confusing a learning goal and a learning experience is easy to do because they both involve student activity. However, experiences and goals play different roles in your course design. Learning experiences build specific skills and proficiencies that support the accomplishment of a larger, more encompassing learning goal. Let's look at a potentially confusing example. In some courses, students produce a portfolio of their work. In this context, a course designer might be tempted to frame the course goal as "Students will assemble a learning portfolio of their work" because it involves a visible, measureable student activity. The fact that the

portfolio process occurs at the end of the course makes it appear even more like a learning goal. However, we say this is a learning experience rather than a learning goal because it is probably a means to an end rather than an end in and of itself. The larger goal emerges from the reason students produce a portfolio in the first place. For us, the portfolio process supports a goal that should look something like this: Students will reflect and summarize (provide supporting evidence) the learning gains they have made throughout the course. Other learning experiences that support this goal may include writing papers, making drawings, or recording teaching videos. As you can see, the learning goal is the terminal behavior that demonstrates the connection of many learning experiences in the course. This pitfall is a violation of the fourth criterion—connectivity.

Pitfall 4: Not Committing to Your Verb

Faculty should avoid choosing higher-level verbs without a willingness to commit to them. The verbs in Bloom's (1956) taxonomy can be powerful. It is often thought that higher-level verbs in the taxonomy are necessary as we move up through the curriculum, or that a course with higher-level verbs is better than a course with lower-level verbs. Some faculty tend to just replace their lower-level-worded intention with higher-level verbs to comply with the criteria for effective course learning goals. Whatever verb you choose, it will have implications down the road for your course design. The higher level the verb you choose, the more proficiencies, learning experiences, and formative assessment will be needed to define the learning pathway. Be clear, and be honest with yourself about your willingness to commit to higher levels of learning.

Up to this point, you have invested a considerable amount of time and brain power into your course's learning goals. You are now ready to list your revised learning goals in Workbox 4.4.

Moving Forward: Choose One of Your Learning Goals

Your set of learning goals probably includes several separate goal statements. The next step in the design process is summative assessment, or measuring the extent to which your students have accomplished a particular goal. The process of designing effective assessment

WORKBOX 4.4.
Your Revised Course Learning Goals

At the end of my course . . .

WORKBOX 4.5.
The Single Course Learning Goal Selected for Subsequent Chapters

At the end of my course . . .

	Exceptional—No improvements needed	Good—Only minor improvements needed	Needs Work—Major improvements needed
LEARNING GOALS	The stated learning goal is written in a way that is **entirely consistent** with the characteristics of effective goals: 1. Is clear and understandable to all 2. Focuses on student performance 3. Requires a high level of thinking that is developmentally appropriate 4. Connects components of the course 5. Is worthwhile and significant	The stated learning goal is written in a way that is **mostly consistent** with the characteristics of effective goals.	The stated learning goal is written in a way that is **substantially inconsistent** with the characteristics of effective goals.
Learning goals are what you want your students to know, feel, or be able to do as a result of taking your course.	Use this space to write any comments/questions you have:		

FIGURE 4.3. The Learning Goals Dimension of Our Course Poster Rubric

instruments considers how a *single* particular learning goal will be measured. Therefore, we ask you to select a learning goal from Workbox 4.4 that you consider to be the most effective goal, one that you think is clear, focuses on student performance, is connective, and requires high levels of thinking. This is an important decision because in the next chapter we take you through the process of producing a summative assessment of this goal. Write the goal you chose in Workbox 4.5, this chapter's culminating workbox. You will work with this goal to identify learning proficiencies in Chapter 6, learning experiences in Chapter 7, and formative assessments in Chapter 8. Once you go through this process with this single goal, you will have the tools and skills necessary to develop your design and course elements for your other goals.

Once you have completed the culminating workbox for this chapter, we encourage you to evaluate your work using the learning goals dimension of our poster evaluation rubric (Figure 4.3). You may also wish to have a campus colleague, a peer, or a friend use the rubric to evaluate your work so far and to help you refine your chosen learning goal before you move on in the course design process.

Note

1. This section represents an updated and revised version of *A Primer on Writing Effective Learning-Centered Course Goals* (Noyd & Staff of the Center for Educational Excellence, 2008).

CHAPTER 5

Summative Assessment

Students' Successful Arrival

AT THIS POINT, YOU'VE established the learning goals that will serve as the foundation for your course and the destination of your learning pathway. In the previous chapter we asked you to pick one specific learning goal to work on, and in this chapter we shift our attention to how you will assess that goal, or how you will know the extent to which your students have arrived at the challenging destination you have set out for them (see Figure 5.1). Our focus is on *summative assessment*, which we define as the tool or set of tools you will use to determine the extent to which your students have achieved your learning goal by the end of the course. At the end of this chapter, we will ask you to identify a summative assessment task that is well aligned with your chosen learning goal.

If you are new to the process of course design, it may seem somewhat odd to think about your course's summative assessment so early in the design process. After all, in the chronology of your course, you and your students aren't likely to encounter the summative assessment until the end of the term, and many other class-related activities (e.g., readings, classroom interactions, homework assignments, etc.) will occur before you arrive at that point. This may explain, at least in part, why so many faculty members choose to put off thinking about their summative assessment until the end of all those other activities.

Asking you to think about your summative assessment now is intentional because we're advocating backward design (Fink, 2003; Wiggins & McTighe, 2005), in which the course design process begins by thinking about what your students will know, be able to do, or feel at the end of your course. This is

why specifying your learning goals is foundational to your course design and why defining your summative assessment is the next step. Before you actually interact with your students, Principle 5 asks you to think about what you'll ask them to do at the end of your course to demonstrate their accomplishment of your learning goal. If the learning goal represents your destination, your summative assessment will represent the tool or tools you'll use to determine the extent to which your students have arrived there.

> Principle 5. An aligned summative assessment will tell you how successfully your students have reached the destination you have set for them.

The most important idea of this chapter is that your summative assessment should be aligned with your learning goals (Biggs, 1996; Cohen, 1987), which means that the actions required to achieve the course learning goal should be the same as those required to succeed on your summative assessment. For example, if your learning goal is for students to be able to create and provide rationale for a five-day weather forecast, then your summative assessment should require students to create the forecast and justify their predictions. This simple idea is critically important to the success of your course. Students dedicate their time and energy doing things that will be assessed, so your choice of a summative assessment will drive your students' behavior. If you want your students to

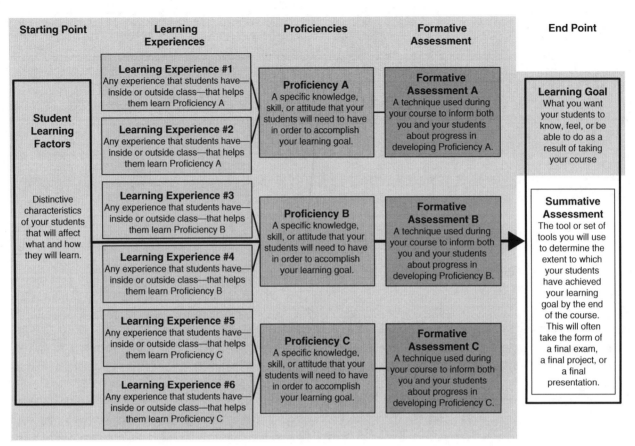

FIGURE 5.1. The Focus of This Chapter Is on Creating a Summative Assessment for Your Selected Learning Goal (unshaded portion of figure)

accomplish a particular learning goal, your summative assessment must align with that goal. To do otherwise would be to lead your students away from the goal you set for their learning.

Unfortunately, faculty members often fail to create summative assessments that are well aligned with their learning goals. According to the National Center for Education Statistics,

Faculty often state that they are seeking to develop students' abilities to analyze, synthesize, and think critically. However, research indicates that faculty do not follow their good intentions when they develop their courses. A formal review and analysis of course syllabi and exams revealed that college faculty do not in reality focus on these advanced skills but instead are more concerned with students' abilities to acquire knowledge, comprehend basic concepts or ideas and terms, and apply basic knowledge. (Walvoord & Anderson, 1998, p. 22)

We've seen this scenario play out in classrooms at our own institution. Several years ago, we observed a general education course taken by first-year students, and in speaking with the faculty teaching the course, it was clear that one of the stated learning goals of the course was to develop students' critical thinking skills. However, when we reviewed the summative assessment (in this course, a final exam), we were struck by the large number of multiple-choice questions focused exclusively on low-level memorization of terminology in the field. It was a clear case of a summative assessment tool that had very little to do with the stated course goal.

This scenario was made all the more troubling when we spoke with some of the students enrolled in the course. One told us that over the course of the semester he had stopped doing the required reading assignments and started tuning out during many of the classroom lessons. When we asked him why, he told us that it became apparent over the course of the semester that his grade would be determined by how well he could memorize the boldfaced terms in the book, not by how well he developed his critical thinking skills. So rather than spend his time developing those skills, he made flash cards of the vocabulary, which for him was the true path to success in the course. Was this student's behavior consistent with the stated course goal of critical thinking? No, it wasn't. Was the student's behavior consistent with the instructors' dreams for his learning in the course? No, it wasn't. But did the student's behavior make sense, given the way that he knew he would be assessed? Yes, it absolutely did.

This anecdote demonstrates why it is so important for you to outline the summative assessment before your course begins. Students generally want to perform well on the summative assessment, and they are likely to adapt their behavior so they can. Your choice of a summative assessment will affect how students spend their time in your course, so why not guide their behavior in ways that are consistent with your stated learning goals?

Step 1: Choose a Course Goal

In general, the first step of creating a summative assessment is choosing a goal to assess. Fortunately, you did that when you chose one goal to focus on at the end of Chapter 4 in Workbox 4.5.

In this chapter our example goal comes from one of our retreat participants, a faculty member in the Air Force Academy's Department of Civil and Environmental Engineering. That goal is stated in the following textbox.

> At the end of my course, students will be able to design embankments and retaining walls.

Step 2: Identify What Students Will Do in an Aligned Assessment

As the overarching principle of this chapter is for your summative assessment to be aligned with your learning goals, the actions required to achieve the course learning goal are the same as the actions required to succeed on your assessment. Table 5.1 shows some examples of what we mean.

Given that our colleague's goal is for students to be able to design embankments and retaining walls, the following textbox shows what students in her course would do in an aligned assessment.

> Students will design embankments and retaining walls.

Use Workbox 5.1 to state what your students will need to do in your aligned assessment. If you do this correctly, your response should be identical to your stated course goal, as illustrated in Table 5.1.

Step 3: Identify an Appropriate Summative Assessment Task

Now we ask you to identify a task that students will perform in the summative assessment. What will you ask students to do to demonstrate their accomplishment of your learning goal and in what context?

You may find it tempting to answer these questions with "take a test" or "write a paper," perhaps because these are assessment tools you have used or experienced most often. However, instead of automatically heading down that path, we ask you to pause. First, simply taking a test or writing a paper isn't sufficiently specific to guide the remainder of your course design. For instance, a written paper as the summative assessment for your course could take on many different forms. Walvoord and Anderson (1998, pp. 193–195) suggest the following assessments, all of which could be broadly construed as written papers:

- Write an annotated bibliography
- Write a client report for an agency
- Write a letter to the editor
- Write a news or feature story
- Write a research proposal addressed to a granting agency
- Write a review of research literature
- Write a technical or scientific report
- Write a term or research paper

Second, besides lacking in specificity, a test or a paper may not necessarily be the best way for you to assess your learning goal. Walvoord and Anderson

TABLE 5.1: Aligning Your Summative Assessment With Your Learning Goal

If your learning goal is	Students will do the following in an aligned assessment:
Students will analyze the causes of the American Civil War.	Students will analyze the causes of the American Civil War.
Given real-world data, students will make a recommendation for a course of action.	Students will be given a set of real-world data pertaining to the course material. Then, using those data, they will make a recommendation for a course of action.
Students will write clear, effective Portuguese.	Students will write clear, effective Portuguese.

WORKBOX 5.1.
Aligned Summative Assessment 1

Your chosen learning goal:	What students will do in an aligned assessment:

(1998, p. 193–195) provide a list of some other ways you could assess your learning goal. This list is not meant to be exhaustive; the number of possible assessment strategies is bounded only by your imagination. We present this relatively short list merely to give you a range of approaches to consider.

- Give a briefing or oral argument
- Present a chart, graph, or visual aid
- Write a computer program
- Build a product (e.g., bridge, rocket, solar panel) to certain specifications
- Engage in a debate
- Solve a mathematical problem
- Write a news or feature story
- Write a poem or play
- Create a work of art, music, architecture, or sculpture

In our course design retreat, some of our faculty participants begin to feel a bit overwhelmed at this point. If they're no longer tied to a test or paper, how do they know what the right option is? How do they choose from among the myriad choices, especially at this relatively early point in the course design process? We admit that this stage of the course design process is as much art as it is science.

The remainder of this chapter offers several guidelines for choosing a summative assessment task. Once you use these guidelines to choose a summative assessment task for your course, we urge you to discuss it with your peers or colleagues to help you refine your thinking and the assessment task you ultimately use in your course.

Alignment

Although we repeatedly stress that your summative assessment must be aligned with your learning goals, it is such an important idea that we've chosen to mention it again. In case our previous discussion wasn't sufficiently compelling, the following is another way to think about alignment. Your choice of a summative assessment serves as what social scientists refer to as an *operational definition* of your course goal; that is, it will be how you measure students' accomplishment of your course goal. If someone asks you how well your students achieved your course goal, you ought to be able to use the results of your summative assessment to inform your answer.

Of course, some learning goals are easier to operationalize than others. If you happen to be working with a high-level learning goal that deals with students' critical thinking skills, for example, a perfect measurement of student accomplishment may be difficult. That's okay, because even if your summative assessment provides imperfect information about your students' achievement of your learning goal, the results of that assessment can still be informative (see Hubbard, 2011). We would much rather you use an imperfect measure that is aligned with your learning goal than use a precise measure of something far less important.

Authenticity

In Chapter 4 we introduced the idea of authentic tasks, which are those in which students face challenges similar to those faced by professionals in the field. Students generally find authentic tasks more motivating than less authentic ones and these tasks are more likely to elicit their best work (Yair, 2000). Therefore, we encourage our own faculty members to choose authentic tasks for their summative assessment as much as possible (see also Huba & Freed, 2000; Wiggins, 1993).

To create an authentic assessment task, think about what professionals in your field do and what they don't do. For example, our colleague from civil and environmental engineering is quick to point out that professional engineers do not spend their time taking multiple-choice tests related to their knowledge of retaining walls. Instead, they are presented with a set of environmental conditions and are then asked to design structures that are appropriate for those conditions. So it would make sense for her to ask students in her class to do something similar: use what they know about engineering principles to design an embankment or retaining wall.

Final Product and the Thought Process

Regardless of the assessment task you choose, students' completion of that task will yield a product of some sort. That product could be relatively simple, such as a series of answers on a written test, or more complex, such as a design for a retaining wall. You will evaluate that product to gauge students' success in meeting your learning goal.

We encourage faculty members to choose an assessment task that leads to a final product and reveals the thought process behind it. In many cases, students' thought processes are what we're ultimately interested in seeing, and the final product is merely a way to reveal those processes. In addition, observing your students' thought processes will also help you learn a great deal more about the quality of their learning. You will be better able to see what they have done correctly, where they have gone astray, and what they could do to improve. This information is invaluable to the students and to you, particularly when you consider revisions to your course. If you notice that your students frequently fall short in a certain area of their thinking, it will point you toward aspects of your course that could be improved when you teach it again in the future.

Returning to our civil engineering colleague, having students design embankments and retaining walls is an aligned and an authentic assessment task. However, those designs may not provide rich information

---

WORKBOX 5.2.
Aligned Summative Assessment 2

What your students need to do in an aligned assessment (from Workbox 5.1):

Your choice of an aligned assessment task:

---

about the thought processes that led to them. Therefore, we recommend asking students to present their rationale for their design choices when they submit their final designs. Doing so would help our colleague better assess what her students were thinking when they made the design decisions.

Weighing Costs and Benefits

All assessments, no matter how simple or complex, have costs for you and your students. Students invest time and energy in preparing for your summative assessment, and they will certainly invest time and energy in completing it. Meanwhile, there are rather significant costs to you in creating a new assessment tool and administering it. Most faculty members are intimately familiar with the costs associated with evaluating students' work that play a role in the choices you ultimately make.

Obviously, the balance of costs and benefits affects the choices made by our civil engineering colleague. In a perfect world, she might want her students to design an embankment and a retaining wall and then test their designs in the field by having the students build them. However, the benefit of field-testing student designs may not justify the substantial costs in time

and money. She may instead ask students to design a structure that could be built but not actually have students build and field-test the design.

Ultimately, our colleague settled on a design project as the aligned summative assessment. To make her assessment authentic, she gave her students real-world situations in which embankments and retaining walls were needed and asked them to use what they learned in the course to create their designs. She chose not to have students actually build any embankments or retaining walls, but she did decide to have students make a presentation of their design projects, allowing her to see their final products and the thinking behind them. This was a good example of an effective summative assessment.

What summative assessment task will you use in your course? Please describe your assessment task in Workbox 5.2, the culminating workbox for this chapter.

Once you have completed Workbox 5.2, we encourage you to evaluate your work using the summative assessment dimension of our course poster rubric, shown in Figure 5.2. If you haven't done so already, you may also wish to ask a colleague to use the rubric to evaluate your work as well.

What About Your Other Learning Goals?

Because you have created a summative assessment for only one of the course goals you generated in Chapter 4, you may be wondering what you should do with the remaining goals. After completing the entire course design process for your first course goal, we would like you to return to your other course goals and work through the design process for those goals as well. If you created three learning goals in Chapter 4, we will ultimately ask you to work through the course design elements three separate times.

This doesn't necessarily mean that your course will have three separate summative assessment tasks. In fact, the very best courses we have come across do not. Instead, we have found that the most clever course designers find ways to create assessment tasks that provide information about more than one learning goal at a time. For instance, our civil engineering colleague's first course goal was for students to design embankments and retaining walls, but an equally important course goal was for them to apply current research in retaining wall design. Her choice of a final assessment is ideally suited for addressing these goals simultaneously. Students' designs and their accompanying explanations can help her assess their achievement of the first course goal, while incorporating the appropriate research into their designs can be used as an assessment of the second goal. In this situation, a single assessment allows the integration of multiple course goals into a single course event.

Looking Ahead: Proficiencies

Once you have described the specific task you will use to assess students' accomplishment of your course goal, we turn our attention to proficiencies—the specific knowledge, skills, and attitudes your students will need to accomplish your learning goals and succeed on your summative assessment. In the next chapter, we demonstrate that identifying these proficiencies will point you toward the knowledge, skills, and attitudes you will need to cultivate in your students once your course begins.

	Exceptional—No improvements needed	Good—Only minor improvements needed	Needs Work—Major improvements needed
SUMMATIVE ASSESSMENT	The summative assessment is *well aligned* with the learning goal.	The summative assessment is *partially aligned* with the learning goal.	The summative assessment is *poorly aligned* with the learning goal.
Summative assessment is the tool or set of tools you will use to determine whether your students have achieved your learning goals by the end of the course. This will often take the form of a final exam, project, or presentation.	Use this space to write any comments/questions you have:		

FIGURE 5.2. The Summative Assessment Dimension of Our Course Poster Rubric

CHAPTER 6

Learning Proficiencies

What Your Students Need to Be Successful

S O FAR IN OUR course design process, you have outlined your student learning factors, course goals, and a summative assessment that is aligned with one of those goals. You can think of your work thus far as articulating the starting point and the ultimate destination of your course. The student learning factors describe who and where your students are at the beginning of your course, the course goals describe where you ultimately want your students to be, and your summative assessment is designed to inform you and your students on the extent to which they've actually arrived there by the end of the course.

In this chapter, you begin to outline the path your students will take as they travel from where they are at the start of your course to where they need to be at the end of it. What knowledge will they need to acquire to successfully achieve your course goal? What skills will they need to develop? What attitudes will they need to possess? We use the term *learning proficiencies*, or simply *proficiencies*, for the specific knowledge, skills, and attitudes your students must have to accomplish your course learning goal (see Figure 6.1).

Determining your learning proficiencies serves a very important function in the course design process. If students acquire all the proficiencies you outline in this chapter, they will be well positioned to succeed on your summative assessment and, consequently, show they have achieved your stated learning goal. Therefore, your task is to help your students develop the proficiencies necessary for them to progress through your course (Principle 6). To do this, you will create learning experiences in Chapter 7, which help students

develop those proficiencies, and formative assessment mechanisms in Chapter 8, which will inform you and your students of the extent to which those proficiencies are being achieved. By outlining your proficiencies in this chapter, you will have established a framework for the remaining choices you have to make in your course design.

> Principle 6. Learning proficiencies lay out the capabilities your students will need to have or acquire to successfully progress along the pathway.

To be honest, many faculty members we work with find the task of outlining their learning proficiencies challenging for two primary reasons. First, many faculty are accustomed to thinking exclusively in terms of the content to be covered in their course (Davis, 2009) rather than in terms of what students have to learn to achieve a course goal. Shifting mind-sets can be challenging for some faculty, especially at this stage of the course design process, when relatively difficult choices may need to be made.

As an example of this first challenge, let's say a faculty member is assigned to teach an introductory course in her discipline. She may not have taught such a course before, but she has certainly taken one. Furthermore, she is also familiar with the content and organization of typical introductory textbooks in the

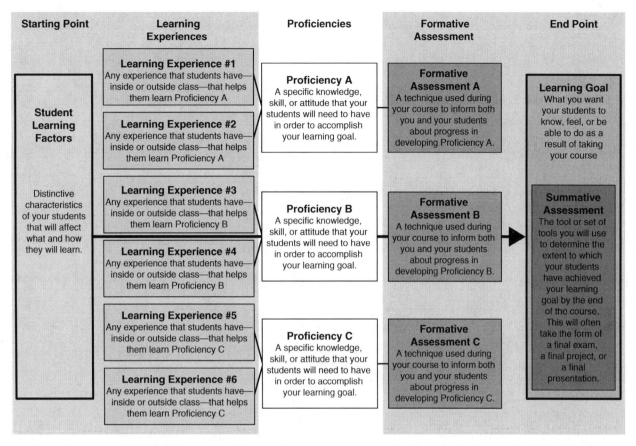

FIGURE 6.1.   The Focus of This Chapter Is on Articulating Proficiencies for Your Selected Learning Goal (unshaded portion of figure)

area, which give her at least some information about what introductory courses usually include. Her familiarity with how the course is normally taught may cause her to include certain aspects of a typical course, even if they aren't particularly well aligned with her own goals for student learning. If this sounds familiar, we remind you to remain focused on your course goals. If you've done a good job writing those goals, and if those goals are reflective of what is most important for your students to learn in your course, then your task at this point is to deconstruct those goals into the specific knowledge, skills, and attitudes needed to accomplish them—even if that takes you down a different path from how the course is normally taught in your discipline.

The second reason is related to the expert blind spot (Ambrose, Bridges, DiPietro, Lovett, Norman, 2010, p. 99). Because of their extensive education

and experience, faculty members are experts in their disciplines, which may cause them to have trouble breaking down their course goals into the fundamental knowledge, skills, and attitudes that lead to them. This makes the task of spelling out learning proficiencies quite difficult, and faculty sometimes overlook some of the most fundamental proficiencies that are important for their students to learn.

Despite these challenges, we have found that faculty members can indeed successfully articulate learning proficiencies for their courses using a step-by-step process. As we dive into that process, we also encourage you to review the list in the next textbox of some general tips you may find helpful as you work through each step. Articulating learning proficiencies is a deeply reflective exercise, and we have found the suggestions in the following textbox helpful in guiding faculty members through the reflection required at each step.

Suggestions for Generating a List of Learning Proficiencies

1. *Reflect on your professional life.* Think about how you perform your course goal in your own professional life. The key is to break down your performance into its component parts. What knowledge, skills, and attitudes do you need to be successful?
2. *Keep a journal as you complete your summative assessment.* Set some time aside to complete the summative assessment in your course. As you complete it, take note of the knowledge, skills, and attitudes that are necessary for you to succeed.
3. *Talk with your peers.* Your peers at your institution or in your professional organizations can be valuable resources in helping you deconstruct the knowledge, skills, and attitudes necessary to achieve the course goal you've created.
4. *Talk with faculty in follow-on courses.* These faculty members look to your course to provide students with certain knowledge, skills, and attitudes. What specifically are they counting on students to have when they arrive at their courses? Answering this question is particularly important if your faculty colleagues notice that students from your class are lacking a proficiency they deem important.
5. *Talk with your students.* This can be especially helpful when your present your students with your course goal for the first time. What obstacles do they foresee? Where do they think they'll get stuck? What knowledge, skills, or attitudes are they apparently lacking when they enter your course that they will need to succeed on your summative assessment?

Identifying Proficiencies for Your Course

In the remainder of this chapter, we take you through a step-by-step process for identifying the learning proficiencies in your course, which includes separate sections on identifying the knowledge, skills, and attitudes necessary for your students to achieve your course goal. Once you have generated these proficiencies, we take you through a sequencing exercise in which you will sort your proficiencies into those that students will encounter early, in the middle, and late in your course. We conclude by asking you to add one final proficiency to your list: the ability to combine all of the proficiencies you've listed in achievement of the course goal. If students have achieved each of your proficiencies and can combine them successfully, they should be well positioned to succeed on your summative assessment and therefore accomplish your course goal.

There are two important keys to success in identifying proficiencies for your course. First, you will want to make sure that the proficiencies you list are individually necessary and collectively sufficient to accomplish your course goal. By indicating that a proficiency is individually necessary, you are stating that students cannot successfully achieve your course goal without having that proficiency. If something isn't necessary to

achieve your course goal, it doesn't need to be in your course. Collectively, your list of proficiencies should also be sufficient to accomplish the course goal. This means that if students acquire all the proficiencies you specify in this chapter, they should be well positioned to succeed on your summative assessment and achieve your course goal. Nothing else should be required for students to be successful.

The second key to success is to write the proficiencies for your course using the same general rules you applied in Chapter 4 to learning goals. Specifically, statements of your proficiencies should begin with the phrase "Students will be able to," and include an action verb that states what students will do to demonstrate their learning of the proficiency. This will make the process of assessing your proficiencies much easier once you begin teaching your course.

As in other chapters, we model each step of our process by walking you through an example from a real course. In this chapter, our example comes from the Probability and Statistics for Engineers and Scientists course in the Department of Mathematical Sciences, a required course for all students pursuing a major in one of the science, technology, engineering, and math (STEM) disciplines at the Air Force Academy. Students typically take this course in their junior year.

Step 1: Focus on a Single Course Goal

The first step in articulating proficiencies is to focus specifically on one of the learning goals you've identified for your course. In the case of the probability and statistics course, the course goal we will use to illustrate our process is shown in the following textbox.

> ### Sample Course Goal
> Given a real-world scenario involving uncertainty, students will be able to apply statistics to recommend an appropriate course of action.

The learning goal you will be working on in this chapter should be the same one you wrote down in Workbox 4.5 and focused on in Chapter 5.

Step 2: Identify Knowledge Proficiencies

To generate knowledge proficiencies, ask yourself what students need to know to accomplish your course goal.[1] Your response will include the facts, concepts, and principles students will ultimately learn in your course (Morrison, Ross, & Kemp, 2001). You are likely to identify knowledge proficiencies by using action verbs in the lower cognitive levels of Bloom's (1956) taxonomy (see Figure 4.2). It is not unusual for faculty members to use words like *describe*, *state*, or *explain* as they write down the knowledge proficiencies for their course.

As you identify the knowledge proficiencies for your course, it is important to be mindful of how students can best organize the knowledge in your course. As an expert in your field, your knowledge is much more than just a random set of facts, concepts, and principles; instead, what you know is organized into rich, coherent structures that help you retrieve your knowledge and see the relationships among the different things you know. Ultimately, your students' learning will be enhanced if their knowledge is similarly built into a coherent organization (National Research Council, 2000).

Mayer (2001) and Ambrose et al. (2010) identify several different kinds of knowledge structures, including the following:

- *Processes* describe how a system works, typically by showing the relationship between its component parts. Processes can often be represented visually in the form of a flow diagram; our course poster template (see Figure 2.3, p. 18) is a flow diagram that represents the various elements of the course design process and how those elements are related to one another.
- *Comparisons* highlight the distinctions between separate concepts. Comparisons can often be represented visually in the form of a matrix that contrasts the characteristics of two or more ideas. A notable example of a comparison is provided by Barr and Tagg (1995), who famously created a matrix comparing the characteristics of the instruction-centered paradigm with the characteristics of the learning-centered one.
- *Classifications* show the categorical relationships between different concepts. Classifications are often represented visually in the form of a hierarchy that demonstrates how specific details can be subsumed by more general rules or principles. Classification hierarchies can be particularly relevant for our statistics professor, as that type of organization helps him to make the most sense of his own knowledge of statistics. That is, his knowledge of specific statistical techniques, such as standard deviation or analysis of variance, is subsumed within broad categories, such as descriptive statistics and inferential statistics. Formalizing this hierarchical knowledge structure in his course helps his students make sense of the disparate knowledge in his field.

The idea of knowledge structures is particularly important for you to consider at this point in the course design process because your students may not necessarily come to your course with the appropriate kinds of structures already in place. As a result, when students encounter the knowledge of your discipline, they may treat it as seemingly random pieces of information. The more you can help your students build coherent knowledge structures, the deeper their learning will ultimately be (Ambrose et al., 2010). Therefore, we encourage you to organize your knowledge proficiencies in a way that mirrors the knowledge structures students must have to achieve your course goal.

Given the hierarchical nature of our statistics professor's knowledge, he found it most helpful to begin the process of identifying knowledge proficiencies by thinking about the major organizing principles students would need to know to use statistics effectively. He then filled in his hierarchy with the more specific concepts and facts students would need to learn in the course. The following textbox shows a subset of knowledge proficiencies that he generated.

Sample Knowledge Proficiencies

Goal: Given a real-world scenario involving uncertainty, students will be able to apply statistics to recommend an appropriate course of action.

Sample knowledge proficiencies:

Principle: Students will be able to recognize assumptions that are made when real-world phenomena are translated into numbers.

Concept: Students will be able to distinguish between descriptive and inferential statistics.

Concept: Students will be able to match appropriate descriptive and inferential statistics to the characteristics of a particular scenario.

Facts: Students will be able to define and describe the characteristics of

- measures of central tendency (e.g., mean, median, mode)
- measures of variability (e.g., variance, standard deviation)
- probability
- random variables and parameters

Even working through this rather limited example should make it clear that articulating all the knowledge proficiencies for your course goal is a sizable job. We urge you to use the strategies referred to earlier in this chapter to help you get started in analyzing your knowledge proficiencies, and we especially encourage you to discuss any questions or concerns with colleagues, peers, or friends.

Now it is your turn. What are the knowledge proficiencies your students need to achieve your chosen course goal? Please write your response to this question in Workbox 6.1.[2]

Step 3: Identify Skill Proficiencies

In addition to knowledge, your students will need skills to successfully meet your course goal. In some cases, physical skills will be needed, such as those described in the psychomotor domain of Bloom's (1956) taxonomy in Appendix B, but more often your students will need a variety of thinking, analytical, or even interpersonal skills to be successful. For example, students may need to be able to construct an essay, solve mathematical problems, use basic laboratory equipment, or work effectively in a team. Regardless of the specific skills in your course, we have found that all academic courses have at least some skills students need to master to be successful.

Given the importance of skills in fostering student success, it is disappointing that so many college classes do not help students develop them (e.g., Arum & Roksa, 2011; Bok, 2006; Keeling & Hersh, 2011). Faculty sometimes lament their students' poor writing, speaking, or teamwork skills instead of making earnest attempts to help students develop them. If your students are lacking the skills necessary for them to be successful in accomplishing your course goals, it is incumbent on you to help students develop those skills. That process begins by examining exactly what those skills are.

Like articulating your knowledge proficiencies, identifying the skills necessary for student success can be a challenging task. To assist you in thinking about the skills that are needed in your course, ask yourself if any of the following are required for your students to meet your course goal:

- specific physical skills (e.g., in a laboratory)
- specific procedures (e.g., for solving problems in your discipline)
- general purpose writing or speaking skills
- critical thinking skills (e.g., critical reading, evaluation of evidence)
- metacognitive skills (e.g., monitoring their own progress)
- interpersonal skills (e.g., working with diverse team members)

After asking the professor of our statistics course to review this list, he generated a subset of skills shown in the following textbox.

WORKBOX 6.1.
Your Knowledge Proficiencies

Goal:

Knowledge proficiencies: *Student will be able to . . .*

Sample Skill Proficiencies

Goal: Given a real-world scenario involving uncertainty, students will be able to apply statistics to recommend an appropriate course of action.

Sample skill proficiencies:

Students will be able to translate real-world phenomena into mathematical terms.

Students will be able to manipulate data and execute statistical functions using Microsoft Excel.

Students will be able to represent statistical results in charts, tables, and graphs that are easy to understand.

Now, list the skill proficiencies students will need in your course in Workbox 6.2.

Step 4: Identify Attitude Proficiencies

Your students will also probably need to have important attitudes to succeed in your course, and if students lack those attitudes, one of your challenges will be to help students develop them. Intentional development of student attitudes is conspicuously absent from many college courses, but we argue that it is just as important as the intentional development of students' knowledge and skills. According to the American Psychological Association (1997), "The rich internal world of thoughts, beliefs, goals, and expectations for success or failure can enhance or interfere with the learner's quality of thinking and information processing" (p. 4). Instructors of the best college courses take a proactive approach in developing these attitudes, not merely expecting students to attain them on their own.

In our experience, three kinds of attitudes are particularly important for students to have or develop in most college classes. The first has to do with motivation—students need to be sufficiently motivated to invest the time and energy necessary to accomplish your course learning goals.[3] Bain (2004) provides several examples of faculty members who have taken intentional strides to address student motivation in their courses. We suggest you do the same, particularly if your course is in an area that does not naturally align with students' academic interests. The student learning factors you identified in Chapter 3 can be useful as you think about including a proficiency related to student motivation.

WORKBOX 6.2.
Your Skill Proficiencies

Goal:

Skill proficiencies: *Student will be able to . . .*

A second important element to consider when outlining attitude proficiencies pertains to students' beliefs about their ability to be successful in your course. Psychologists (e.g., Bandura, 1997) refer to people's beliefs about their ability to be successful as *self-efficacy*, and research indicates it can play a key role in determining student success. For example, students with high levels of self-efficacy have been shown to spend more time and effort on learning activities (Bassi, Steca, Delle Fave, & Vittorio Caprara, 2007) and are more likely to persist when confronted with difficult tasks than students with low self-efficacy (Pintrich & De Groot, 1990). Therefore, it would be wise to consider building the development of students' self-efficacy into your course.[4] This may be especially true if your course is designed for students who may be new to your discipline or whose academic backgrounds are particularly weak.

Finally, a third idea to consider when developing attitude proficiencies has to do with students' willingness to work with ideas that may challenge their current ways of thinking. For instance, consider the insights that emerge from Kitchener and King's (1981, 2004) reflective judgment model. According to the model, students in late adolescence and adulthood progress through of series of developmental phases regarding how they think about ill-structured problems. Many beginning students are likely to show signs of *prereflective thinking* in which they assume that knowledge is certain and any question has a single correct answer. Not surprisingly, these students may struggle when faced with uncertainty. To succeed, they need plenty of support from you, and they also must be willing to face uncertain situations and become comfortable when those situations challenge their epistemic assumptions. For your course to succeed, you may need to foster the development of students' attitudes in this regard.

Upon reflecting on these issues, our probability and statistics instructor identified the attitudes shown in the following textbox as necessary for students to succeed in his course.

Sample Attitude Proficiencies

Goal: Given a real-world scenario involving uncertainty, students will be able to apply statistics to recommend an appropriate course of action.

Sample attitude proficiencies:

Students will be motivated to solve real-world scenarios involving uncertainty.

Students will believe they can solve real-world scenarios successfully.

Students will be comfortable recommending courses of action, even in the face of probabilistic information.

Now it is time to turn your attention to your course. In general, what attitudes will students need to meet your course goal? Will students have to be highly motivated to succeed in your course? Will students need high self-efficacy? Will you challenge your students' thinking in such a way that they will need to approach your discipline with an actively open mind? If you answer yes, then you need to include these attitudes in your list of proficiencies. In the next chapters, we discuss how to build these proficiencies and determine if students have the level of proficiency they need to be successful. Please write your responses to these questions in Workbox 6.3 (see Appendix B for a description of the affective domain and its associated verbs).

Step 5: Review or Revise Your Lists of Proficiencies

As noted by Nilson (2010), students will need to accomplish some of the proficiencies earlier in the learning process than others. Therefore, the next step is to combine your lists of knowledge, skill, and attitude proficiencies and order them. Doing so will help both you and your students see the path they will be taking as they navigate through your course.[5]

We encourage you to begin the sequencing process by identifying the most fundamental proficiencies, those developed in the early stages of your course. Next, you can consider those proficiencies that are more intermediate, those developed in the middle part of your course. Finally, think about the proficiencies that tend to be developed later or near the end of the course and that build on what students have accomplished earlier. In reality, your students' development of your learning proficiencies is unlikely to follow this strict linear sequence, and in fact many of our most successful colleagues have at least introduced students to relatively complex proficiencies quite early in their courses. Nonetheless, this general framework can still be helpful for organizing your proficiencies into a meaningful sequence.

WORKBOX 6.3.
Your Attitude Proficiencies

Goal:

Attitude proficiencies: *Student will be able to . . .*

Please review the lists you've created and revise them where appropriate. Better yet, now would be a good time to ask your peers to review your lists with you. Even those who are one step removed from your course are highly likely to come up with ideas that may have escaped you until now.

Now is also a good time to consider whether your students already possess any of the proficiencies on your lists. Some students may already have or at least have a reasonable base for possessing some of your listed proficiencies. For instance, students at our institution are generally technically savvy and have extensive experience manipulating data in Microsoft Excel even before they arrive in the junior-level probability and statistics course. With this in mind, our statistics professor may wish to revise his second skill proficiency so that it focuses less on data manipulation in Excel, which his students already have experience with, and more on using specific statistical functions that will be new to them. The following is a possible revision:

> *Original skill proficiency: Students will be able to manipulate data and execute statistical functions using Microsoft Excel.*

> *Revised skill proficiency: Students will be able to execute statistical functions using Microsoft Excel.*

If your students possess any of the proficiencies on your lists, you may wish to revise your lists to focus on the knowledge, skills, and attitudes they don't already have. If you are certain your students already possess one or more of the proficiencies you've generated, those proficiencies can be deleted.

On the other hand, it is likely that at least some the proficiencies will be completely new to your students, and they will have to build the necessary knowledge, skills, or attitudes completely from scratch. For example, there is no reason for our statistics professor to believe that his students will come to class familiar with terminology such as *random variables* or *parameters*, as students will not likely have encountered those terms in previous courses. As a result, he will need to keep those proficiencies on his list, written as he had originally generated them.

As you reflect on what your own students' knowledge, skills, and attitudes will be when they enter your course, it is once again helpful to refer to the work in Chapter 3 on student learning factors. In addition, for a realistic perspective, we encourage you to ask faculty colleagues in your department what students are apt to be like. If you are still uncertain, we recommend collecting information about your students' proficiencies in the form of a formative assessment (see Chapter 8) during the early portion of your course.

Step 6: Sequence Your List of Proficiencies

Three disparate lists of knowledge, skill, and attitude proficiencies won't define a very useful pathway for your course, so combining your lists and putting them into some semblance of order is necessary. We encourage you to begin by identifying the most foundational proficiencies, those developed in the early stages of your course. Next, you can consider those proficiencies that are more intermediate, those developed in the middle part of your course. Finally, think about the proficiencies that tend to be developed later or near the end of the course and that build on what students have accomplished earlier. In reality, your students' development of your learning proficiencies is unlikely to follow this strict linear sequence, and in fact many of our most successful colleagues have at least introduced students to relatively complex proficiencies quite early in their courses. Nonetheless, this general framework can still be helpful for organizing your proficiencies into a meaningful sequence.

As a model, let's return to the probability and statistics course. In the following textbox, we have rewritten the proficiencies generated earlier in the chapter, but we have mixed the proficiencies from the knowledge, skill, and attitude categories and sorted them in a meaningful order. The foundational proficiencies pertain largely to student attitudes as well as to the fundamental knowledge and skills needed to represent real-world problems in numerical terms. The intermediate proficiencies relate to the knowledge and skills associated with the use of descriptive and inferential statistics, including executing appropriate statistical functions in Microsoft Excel. The most complex proficiencies pertain to students' ability to interpret the results of their statistical analyses, to represent those results in an appropriate format, and to be comfortable making recommendations on the basis of probabilistic information. Organized in this way, we hope you can see a pathway start to emerge

An Example of Sequenced Proficiencies

Goal: Given a real-world scenario involving uncertainty, students will be able to apply statistics to recommend an appropriate course of action.

Early proficiencies:

Attitude: Students will be motivated to solve real-world scenarios involving uncertainty.

Attitude: Students will believe that they can solve real-world scenarios successfully.

Skill: Students will be able to translate real-world phenomena into mathematical terms.

Knowledge: Students will be able to recognize assumptions that are made when real-world phenomena are translated into numbers.

Middle proficiencies:

Knowledge: Students will be able to define and describe the characteristics of

- measures of central tendency (e.g., mean, median, mode)
- measures of variability (e.g., variance, standard deviation)
- probability
- random variables and parameters

Knowledge: Students will be able to distinguish between descriptive and inferential statistics.

Knowledge: Students will be able to match appropriate descriptive and inferential statistics to the characteristics of a particular scenario.

Skill: Students will be able to execute statistical functions using Microsoft Excel.

Late proficiencies:

Skill: Students will be able to interpret the real-world implications of their statistical results.

Skill: Students will be able represent statistical results in charts, tables, and graphs that are easy to understand.

Attitude: Students will be comfortable recommending courses of action, even in the face of probabilistic information.

for what students will be doing at various stages of this particular course.

Now we ask you to sequence the proficiencies in your course. Using an approach similar to the one taken by our statistics professor, sort your proficiencies into three categories of early, middle, and late, and write your responses in Workbox 6.4.

Step 7: Pull All the Proficiencies Together

Before we move on to the next stage of our course design process, we would like you to add one final proficiency to the list you generated in Workbox 6.4—students need to be able to combine all proficiencies by demonstrating their accomplishment of the learning goal. We used to think that it was sufficient for course designers to deconstruct their learning goals into the individual proficiencies that made them up and that students would be well positioned to succeed if they could simply master each one. When we implemented such a system in our own classes, however, it became immediately clear that there is something about achieving the larger learning goal that is not captured by the mere collection of deconstructed proficiencies; the whole is somehow greater than the sum of its parts. Therefore, it is necessary to add a synthesizing or integrative proficiency so that students learn how to pull together everything you've identified in

---

WORKBOX 6.4.
Your Sequenced Proficiencies

Goal:

Early proficiencies: *Students will be able to . . .*

Middle proficiencies: *Students will be able to . . .*

Late proficiencies: *Students will be able to . . .*

---

this chapter to demonstrate their accomplishment of the learning goal.

From a practical standpoint, the inclusion of this final synthesizing or integrative proficiency will become important as you move forward in developing learning experiences (Chapter 7) and opportunities for formative assessment (Chapter 8). In short, an important part of your course will be dedicated to letting students practice performing the complete task associated with your learning goal and providing them with feedback about their performance of that task. This is very much in keeping with Bain's (2004) observation that learning occurs best when students are given the chance to try, fail, and receive feedback, all before

encountering a summative assessment that will be used to make a formal statement (often in the form of a grade) about the students' learning.

So what does this mean for the professor of the probability and statistics course we've been illustrating in this chapter? In keeping with the idea of an aligned summative assessment, this professor has a final exam in which he gives students a real-world scenario and asks them to apply statistics to recommend an appropriate course of action. We are suggesting that the final exam will not be the first time students have the chance to demonstrate their accomplishment of the course goal. Instead, we recommend that the course include some specific learning experiences dedicated to helping students pull together what they've learned to complete the whole task, some assessment of how well they are able to do it, and an opportunity for students to receive feedback on their performance before the final exam. By taking this approach, our professor puts his students in the very best position to succeed on the summative assessment, thereby demonstrating their accomplishment of the overall course goal. We urge you to adopt a similar approach in guiding your students toward your course goal.[6]

Step 8: Looking Ahead

In this chapter, you have articulated all the learning proficiencies your students will need to be successful in meeting your larger course goal. Taken together, these proficiencies mark the pathway for you and your students, and they are also critical to the rest of

your course design, particularly as you consider learning experiences (Chapter 7) and formative assessment (Chapter 8).

The proficiencies you have identified will play a role in the design of your course, and you will eventually need to identify learning experiences and formative assessments for each of them. However, for the sake of creating your course poster and simplifying the work you will do in Chapters 7 and 8, we encourage you to focus on a subset of those proficiencies for now. Specifically, we ask you to list no more than four proficiencies (one each from early, middle, and late in the course, as well as the final proficiency that pulls all of the other proficiencies together) in Workbox 6.5, the culminating workbox for this chapter. These are the proficiencies you will be working on in Chapters 7 and 8, and they will be included in your course poster. Use the proficiencies dimension of our course poster rubric in Figure 6.2 to evaluate the contents of Workbox 6.5.

	Exceptional—No improvements needed	Good—Only minor improvements needed	Needs Work—Major improvements needed
PROFICIENCIES	You have identified the ***most important proficiencies*** necessary for students to accomplish the learning goal. Your poster reflects the most important knowledge, skills, and attitudes students will need to learn in your course.	You have identified ***some of the important proficiencies*** necessary for students to accomplish the learning goal. You may wish to look at your list again to ensure that you include the most important proficiencies on your poster.	You have ***left out the most important proficiencies*** necessary for students to accomplish the learning goal. Please look at your list again to ensure that you include the most important proficiencies on your poster.
Proficiencies are the specific knowledge, skills, and attitudes your students need to accomplish your learning goals (and therefore to succeed on the summative assessment of the goals).	Use this space to write any comments/questions you have:		

FIGURE 6.2. The Proficiencies Dimension of Our Course Poster Rubric

---

WORKBOX 6.5
The Proficiencies You Will Use in Chapters 7 and 8

Goals:

An early proficiency: *Students will be able to . . .*

Proficiency A
A middle proficiency: *Students will be able to . . .*

Proficiency B
A late proficiency: *Students will be able to . . .*

Proficiency C
Pulling them all together: *Students will be able to . . .*

Notes

1. Note the difference between this question and the questions, What do I, the professor, know about this topic? or What topics are covered in my favorite textbook? We've purposefully phrased this question to keep you focused on what is necessary to accomplish your course goal.
2. In each of the workboxes in this chapter, we ask you to rewrite your learning goal. This may seem redundant, but writing it out each time keeps the learning goal at the forefront of the decisions you make. This will help ensure that your proficiencies are aligned directly with your learning goals.
3. Discussion of student motivation is closely related to the caring dimension in Fink's (2003) taxonomy of significant learning.
4. One way to build self-efficacy is to give students a taste of success relatively early in your course. Once you've identified some of the most fundamental proficiencies, create ways for students to see their progress in developing those proficiencies.
5. Nilson (2007) advocates that course designers share the results of this sequencing activity with students by using a "graphic syllabus" and an "outcomes map." As you will see in Chapter 9, we similarly recommend sharing your final course poster with students, as doing so will make the learning pathway you've built clearer for them.
6. When we make this argument with our own colleagues, someone inevitably raises a concern about us encouraging faculty to teach the test. We address this concern, as well as several others, in Chapter 11.

CHAPTER 7

Learning Experiences

Traveling the Pathway

THIS CHAPTER TAKES YOU through a part of the design process that is perhaps the most familiar to you: learning experiences (see Figure 7.1). If you are like many college faculty, you have planned your classes using particular teaching techniques or methods, such as lectures, class discussions, collaborative learning activities, demonstrations, or laboratory experiments. In our experience, an emphasis on using a specific teaching technique leads faculty to look at these activities from a teaching-centered perspective. They ask themselves what *they* will do, what topics *they* will cover, how *they* will organize the course material. Everything is focused on what the teacher will do. This mind-set leads them to emphasize what they do to students and reinforces the misconception that the way to improve student learning is through the use of a particular technique alone. Decades of learning research and our own experience tell us that student learning is very complex, and how we teach, while important, is only one of several factors involved in determining what students ultimately learn.

> Principle 7. Learning doesn't depend on what is done to your students but instead on how they interpret their experiences.

One of the hallmarks of our philosophy and course design process is to take the perspective of the learner, or student, which brings us to Principle 7, shown in the preceding textbox. This principle is framed in a learning-centered mind-set in which your lesson plans create learning experiences for your students, and the questions you ask yourself shift in perspective as well, for example,

- What will students do in this lab?
- What kinds of thinking will students have to do to succeed on this project?
- What will the students experience from your lecture?
- In what ways will students be cognitively engaged in the class discussion?
- How will students be motivated to learn by your demonstration?
- What misconceptions will steer students in the wrong direction in solving this type of problem?

When framed as learning experiences, classroom activities are planned and implemented in a deliberate and intentional way to promote student learning. In our design process we define a *learning experience* as something a student does, physically or mentally, that changes their knowledge, skills, or attitudes. Learning experiences occur in our classes when students interact with their peers, listen to our lectures, participate in discussions, or work in small groups, but they also occur outside class when students participate in literature searches, write papers, read textbooks, take online quizzes, or solve problems. Regardless of when and where learning experiences occur, their purpose is stated in Principle 8 in the following textbox.

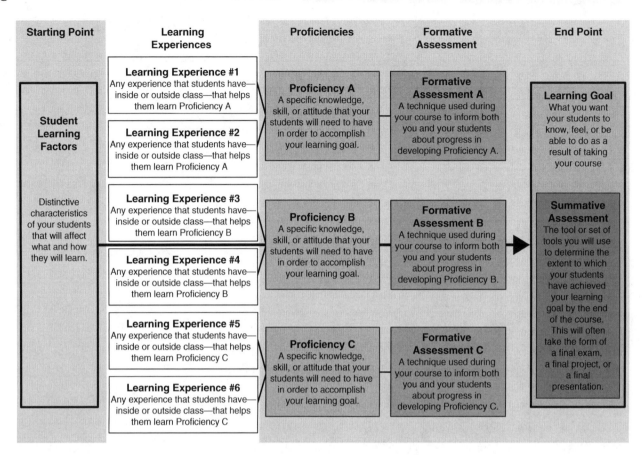

FIGURE 7.1. The Focus of This Chapter Is on Planning Learning Experiences for Your Selected Learning Goal (unshaded portion of figure)

Principle 8. Effective learning experiences will help your students develop necessary learning proficiencies.

In this book, we present the elements of course design in the order we think you should plan your course, starting with student learning factors and then developing learning goals and summative assessments and so on. However, this is not how students encounter your course; they do this through the learning experiences you design. The main task of this chapter, as shown in Figure 7.2, is to assemble a sequence of learning experiences that intentionally build the necessary and sufficient proficiencies developed in Chapter 6, so that students will accomplish the stated learning goal (Chapter 4) and perform successfully on your summative assessment (Chapter 5). To model this task, we use an example from a plant biology course shown in the following textbox.

Course Goal and Proficiencies for a Plant Biology Course

Learning goal: Students will identify an unknown plant using a field guide.

A sequence of proficiencies:

1. Early: Describe the form and arrangement of leaves on a plant.
2. Early: Describe and name the parts of a typical flower.
3. Middle: Observe and point out the parts of leaves and flowers in nature.
4. Middle: Be aware, open, and comfortable with the variation between plants in nature and the figures in the field guide.
5. Late: Use a field guide to identify a known plant and an unknown plant.

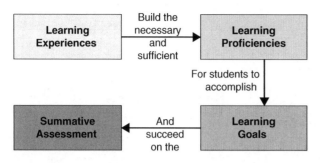

FIGURE 7.2. The Relationship of Learning Experiences to Other Components of the Course Design Process

This task has three steps: Generate a list of possible learning experiences, explore the characteristics of each of the learning experiences on your list, and match appropriate learning experiences with each of the proficiencies identified in the previous chapter. The result of your work in this chapter will be a list of learning experiences that are well aligned with the proficiencies identified in Chapter 6.

Step 1: Brainstorm Possible Learning Experiences

To start off, think of as many types of learning experiences as you can and write them in Workbox 7.1. List the learning experiences that occur in the classes you teach or in classes you have taken as a student. To ensure that you're appropriately focused on your students, be sure to begin all the learning experiences with a verb that indicates what students will be doing during the experience. In the following textbox, we've included a small number of appropriately phrased examples to help get you started.

It is important to note that some learning techniques involve several different learning experiences. In this case, it is necessary to break down the technique into parts to describe what students are experiencing during the activity. For example, listing a jigsaw activity (Barkley, Cross, & Major, 2005; Millis, 2010) in the workbox needs further elaboration by specifying that students interact with others in small groups, research a topic, and then teach others about that topic. Thus, this cooperative learning technique involves at least three different learning experiences. Finally, brainstorming is a list-generating activity that does not evaluate the ideas, it just gets them out and down on paper to be considered later (i.e., in Step 2).

Example Brainstorming Related to a Plant Biology Course

Students

1. Listen to a face-to-face lecture
2. Listen to a podcast
3. Participate in a discussion
4. Watch a demonstration
5. Read the textbook and look at the accompanying illustrations
6. Create a Venn diagram
7. Enter data into a spreadsheet
8. Take an online quiz (select answers to questions)

As you examine your list of learning experiences, you probably realize that like most of us you have a limited repertoire of learning experiences to choose from. The set of experiences we use in our courses is often limited by how we were taught or what we did as students, which for most of us was the lecture-based, instructional delivery model. On the other hand, choosing from a wider range of learning experiences gives you the power to better align a particular learning experience with the proficiency you want students to build. To expand the set of possible learning experiences you can use in your course, we encourage you to discuss alternative methods with colleagues on your campus. In our course design retreat, an individual faculty, member will typically generate less than a dozen learning experiences, but when he or she consults with other faculty, the resulting list can contain over 50 different types of experiences. The community of instructors and course designers often benefit from a larger toolbox to guide student accomplishment of specific learning goals.

Step 2: Characterize the Capabilities and Constraints of Learning Experiences

It may be helpful to view your brainstormed list of learning experiences as your teaching toolbox; each tool is particularly well suited to help students accomplish a particular task. In this way, each of the learning experiences in Workbox 7.1 has a set of particular characteristics and capabilities that help students acquire

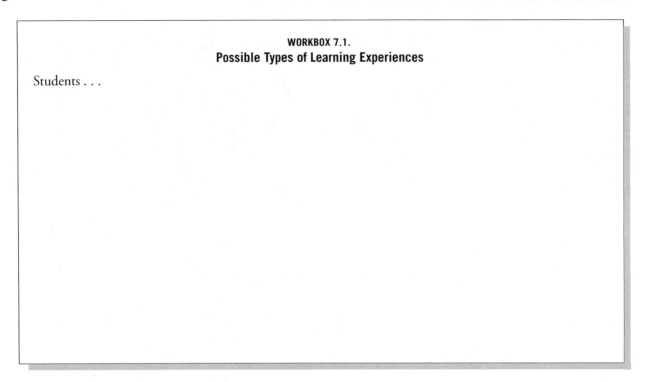

WORKBOX 7.1.
Possible Types of Learning Experiences

Students . . .

specific learning proficiencies. For example, some of the advantages of listening to a podcast include convenience and portability; students can listen to it when they are mentally alert and in a convenient place. They can listen to it multiple times at whatever pace suits them. Podcasts also allow students to target areas of lectures that are confusing or unclear. On the downside, podcasts do not allow for student interaction or provide students with feedback on their learning; they are simply tools designed to transmit bodies of information. Other learning experiences serve this same function, such as reading a textbook or listening to a lecture. Therefore, before you begin to figure out which learning experience is the most appropriate for the proficiencies you are trying to build in Step 3, it is necessary to consider the characteristics (we categorize these as *strengths, weaknesses,* and *constraints*; see Table 7.1) of each learning experience. This is your task in this step.

Before you begin, let's further define a *constraint.* Practical constraints may force you to choose a learning experience that is less than your optimal choice. For example, if you wanted students to identify flowers from a variety of habitats (e.g., deserts, rain forests, etc.), you might have them visit a botanical garden with a worldwide collection of plants. In many cases this learning experience is not possible for the entire class; it's constrained by cost, travel, or time. However,

alternative experiences may be more reasonable, such as viewing images or doing library research. Other practical constraints include teacher preparation time, student workload, lack of equipment, or technology.

In this step we ask you to pull a subset of the learning experiences from Workbox 7.1 and describe their capabilities as well as their possible constraints in Workbox 7.2. Table 7.1 contains examples from a plant biology course, along with references for more information.

Once you have accomplished this step, set it aside and return to the learning proficiencies at the conclusion of Chapter 6. Our next step will be to match these proficiencies with the learning experiences that will help students accomplish them.

Step 3: Match Proficiencies to Learning Experiences

Now is the time for you to get to the heart of what a learning experience does for your students: builds proficiencies—the knowledge, skills, and attitudes necessary to accomplish the learning goal. While many different learning experiences will help students learn any given proficiency, how do you select the best learning experience?

TABLE 7.1: Characteristics of Learning Experiences

Learning Experience	Strengths: How It Helps Learning	Weaknesses and Constraints	Reference
Listen to a lecture or podcast.	Orally transmits organized information about a particular topic efficiently	Often not very engaging for students; students generally passive; requires listening skills and focused attention	Bligh (2000)
Participate in a class discussion.	Engages students in dialogue and critical thinking	Takes large amount of class time; difficult with large classes; unpredictable	Brookfield (2005)
Take part in a laboratory experience: dissection.	Practical; hands on; stimulates curiosity and observation in a skill, process, or event; makes abstract concepts more concrete; models a skill	Time to set up and obtain materials; may make skill look easier than it is	Ahmad (2012)
Take an online quiz.	Exposes students to vocabulary terms and their definitions, builds and tests factual knowledge, provides immediate feedback, completed on student's time, out of class	Tends to fragment knowledge into pieces rather than show students the concept relationships	Dobson (2008)

WORKBOX 7.2.
Characteristics of Learning Experiences

Learning Experience (from Workbox 7.1)	Strengths: How It Helps Learning	Weaknesses and Constraints

How to Select Effective Learning Experiences

Selecting the most meaningful learning experiences involves trade-offs in which you gain some learning benefits while giving up others or minimize some constraints while accepting others. With all things considered, we choose learning experiences that combine and balance the following characteristics:

- Aligned: The experience directly supports and leads to the accomplishment of the proficiency and learning goal.
- Engaging: The experience encourages students to spend the time necessary to focus, concentrate, and successfully complete the learning task.
- Well-supported: The experience adequately supports students with the resources (i.e., textbooks, classroom notes, instructor assistance) necessary to help them successfully complete the task or experience.
- Efficient: The experience has large learning benefits relative to the constraints; students' becomes more proficient, more knowledgeable, more skilled, or more demonstrative of the attitudes you desire with fewer or less intense constraints, such as class time, student time, preparation time, and cost of resources.

Even with these qualities, a learning experience can be quickly undermined if students' perceptions are not fully taken into account. First, students need to be clear on how to complete the task and on the purpose of the activity, and they must easily see how the task leads to the particular proficiency they are working to accomplish. Overly complex learning experiences diminish clarity by placing an added burden on students to understand and follow instructions (Marcus, Cooper, & Sweller, 1996), and they take time away from the learning task. Second, students also need to feel safe if they fail and make mistakes in a low-stakes environment. After all, the purpose of the experience is to help them develop learning proficiencies and guide them along the pathway of your course to the higher-stakes summative assessment farther down the road.

Let's now apply these criteria to an early learning proficiency in the plant biology class: *Students will describe and name the parts of a typical flower.* It is important to clarify that the verb *describe* means that the student will represent by a figure, model, picture, or words the form, parts, and the relationship of the parts of an object, in this case a typical flower. Recognizing and naming the parts of a flower is essential to achieving the goal. This proficiency could be supported by a variety of learning experiences in which students listen to a lecture or a podcast; use a computer mouse to select, drag, and drop a name into its proper place on a diagram; make a physical model of a flower; draw a flower and then label it; or label a diagram of a flower. Which learning experience best balances the criteria for an effective learning experience? Face-to-face lectures are very efficient, but as with a podcast, students are passive observers of the instructor doing the bulk of the thinking.[1] Also, students come to the course already familiar with the concept of a flower, so they do not need direct instruction at this stage. The drag-and-drop, model-building, drawing, and labeling experiences are much more engaging. However, model building comes with higher upfront costs, such as time, materials, complexity, and instructor guidance. Similarly, a drag and drop activity requires the skills to build the activity and then post it on a website. Giving students a flower diagram to label is well aligned because it is similar to the learning goal they will be asked to perform. Also, students are supported by a textbook for reference to complete the task. This experience has few constraints, and the task is simple and easy to understand, which is especially useful early in the sequence.

It's always important to keep in mind that a single learning experience may not build the proficiency in its entirety; sometimes the proficiency is accomplished through a combination of learning experiences that work together in a particular sequence.

Aligning and Sequencing Learning Experiences

Let's return to our plant identification example for our alignment task. Table 7.2 shows that the learning goal is supported by five proficiencies from the early, middle, and late phases of the learning process, which moves the acquisition of cognitive skills from simple to more complex problem solving (Anderson, 1982; VanLehn, 1996). The first two proficiencies involve knowledge, the third and fifth proficiency are skills, and the fourth proficiency involves an attitude.

The right-hand column shows the specific learning experiences that build these particular proficiencies. Field guides generally use flowers and leaves in the identification process. Therefore, Proficiencies 1 and 2 require students to be able to observe and describe basic flower and leaf forms. Students become proficient by reading and labeling a diagram of flower parts

TABLE 7.2: Align Learning Goal With Proficiencies and With Learning Experiences

Learning Goal: Students will identify an unknown plant using a field guide.

Sequence of Proficiencies Students will	*Learning Experience* Students will
1. Early: Describe and name the parts of a typical flower.	Label a diagram of flower parts.
2. Early: Describe the form and arrangement of leaves on a plant.	Label a diagram of common leaf forms and their arrangement on a plant.
3. Middle: Observe and point out the parts of leaves and flowers in nature.	Watch instructor point out parts on a complex flower.
	Dissect a flower.
	Observe and characterize different leaf forms and arrangements.
4. Middle: Students will be aware, open, and comfortable with variations of plants in nature between their specimen and the figures in the field guide.	Watch instructor point out how a plant varies from figures shown in the field guide.
5. Late: Use a field guide to identify a known plant and then an unknown plant.	Listen to an explanation of how to use a field guide.
	Use a field guide to identify a known simple plant and then an unknown plant.

and leaf forms from their textbook. This simple low-level learning experience is easily accomplished outside class as a student assignment.

Proficiency 3 requires students to apply their book knowledge to a plant from nature. They watch a demonstration before embarking on a flower dissection on their own. This assumes that students are proficient with the use of forceps and a dissecting microscope. Also, a learning experience does not have to take up an entire lesson or class period; the flower dissection could be a 20–30 minute activity. Proficiency 3 can also move students from simple flowers similar to those shown in the text to more complex flowers in nature that show variations on the basic plan (i.e., petals form a tube rather than a leaflike form, some parts are lacking, etc.). This intermediate proficiency is supported by and built from earlier learning experiences that build students' vocabulary (discerning flower parts and matching terms) and visual literacy by watching the instructor point out the parts.

Many course designers tend to overlook attitude proficiencies and the accompanying learning experiences that develop them. They often see attitudes as by-products of other experiences. However, in our design model all proficiencies need to be intentionally developed and supported through learning experiences. In our example in Table 7.2, Proficiency 4 requires students to become aware of and be open to the fact that plants in nature do not always conform to the figures and photos in the field guide; students without this attitude often become frustrated with the process. Knowing this is an important proficiency, the instructor can make students aware of differences by pointing out several examples of how plants in nature vary from the prototype shown in the field guide.

This example shows a gradual strategy to move students from simple, more concrete tasks in the early phase to more complex tasks in the middle and late phases of the goal. The fifth and final proficiency pulls together the previous proficiencies in a synthesis type

WORKBOX 7.3.
Align Learning Goal With Proficiencies and With Learning Experiences

Learning goal:

Sequence of Proficiencies	Learning Experience

of authentic learning experience in which students begin to become proficient in using a field guide and making decisions about the flower and leaf characteristics of their unknown plant. Notice that the final proficiency is similar to the learning goal itself and represents a critical step in the learning process.

Now that we have modeled the task, it is your turn to match the learning experiences you listed in Workbox 7.2 (or add others) with the sequence of learning proficiencies you listed in the final workbox in Chapter 6 (Workbox 6.5). The challenge is to structure learning so that students receive adequate opportunities to build their proficiency through practice. It is especially effective to build and then reinforce the same proficiency through a variety of learning experiences (Ambrose et al., 2010).

Your deliverable at this step is Workbox 7.3, the culminating workbox for this chapter. In this workbox you will restate your learning goal from Chapter 4 and then list your proficiencies from Chapter 6 in the first column. Then, choose the appropriate supporting learning experiences from Workbox 7.2 and put them in the right column. Do not be constrained by the table's rows, simply add rows as you see fit and merge

rows when more than one learning experience aligns with and supports a particular proficiency.

Step 4: Evaluate the Sufficiency of Your Learning Experiences

Before moving on to the final element of our course design process, we ask you to pause to review the logic of what you have accomplished in this chapter. Your task has been to match each of the proficiencies you generated in Chapter 6 with learning experiences designed to help students achieve them. If done well, this process has helped outline many of the day-to-day details of your course. If students achieve your proficiencies, they should be well positioned to succeed on your summative assessment (Chapter 5), which will serve as an indication that students have met your learning goal (Chapter 4). The approach you've applied is intentionally designed to promote student learning and success.

The effectiveness of your work in this chapter rests on the assumption that the learning experiences you outlined are sufficient to help students achieve the desired proficiencies. Therefore, the final step is to evaluate the sufficiency of the learning experiences you've generated in this chapter. If your collection of learning experiences is indeed sufficient, then you are ready to proceed; if it is not, then this is the time to revise your list. It is far better to make adjustments now than to be surprised by students who are unprepared for success later on.

For a number of reasons, developing student proficiencies can be more difficult than it might initially seem. For instance, research shows that students' prior knowledge affects their learning of new information (Ambrose et al., 2010). In some cases, however, students' knowledge about your course material may be inaccurate or incomplete. To build knowledge proficiencies, it may be necessary for you to identify gaps or misconceptions in your students' existing knowledge and provide supplementary learning experiences to help account for them. Ambrose et al. (2010) provide a number of excellent suggestions for learning experiences that are helpful in these situations, such as asking students to make and test predictions based on their preexisting beliefs. By testing those beliefs explicitly, students will be more likely to discover the ways their prior knowledge may be faulty.

As noted in Chapter 6, your knowledge of your course content is likely to be organized in meaningful cognitive structures that your students probably lack (National Research Council, 2000). So while you may grasp the organization of your discipline, your students may experience your course material, at least initially, as nothing more than a series of isolated, unrelated facts. To combat that problem, you may need to be explicit about helping your students learn how experts in your field organize their knowledge. This takes time and effort on your part, but it is needed for your students to fully develop the knowledge proficiencies you've outlined.

As with physical skills, the development of cognitive skills (such as evaluation or analysis) requires substantial practice and feedback (Ambrose et al., 2010), which means your students are unlikely to become proficient at your higher-level skills by completing a single lesson or assignment. If your skill proficiencies include these sorts of high-level thinking skills, we encourage you to build in multiple opportunities for your students to practice their skills, receive feedback on their performance, and then try again (Bain, 2004). You will need to be intentional about building these opportunities into your course.

Finally, pay careful attention to the development of any attitude proficiencies you've identified for your course. Changing students' attitudes and their beliefs about themselves won't happen overnight. Therefore, we encourage you to include multiple experiences to address your attitude proficiencies for the entirety of your course. For instance, if you are teaching students who have doubts about their ability to be successful in your discipline, it may be necessary to scaffold the work they do so that they encounter at least some measure of success early in your course. We have also found it useful to be overt about the design of our courses and to show students the pathway they can follow to success. Too often we've found that students' negative beliefs about their abilities in a particular area of study are caused at least in part by the inability of faculty members to show students what it means to succeed and what students need to do to get there.

The bottom line of this discussion is that developing knowledge, skill, or attitude proficiencies may be more difficult than you initially believe. Therefore, it is important for you to take a close look at the learning experiences you've generated in this chapter to ensure that they are sufficient to achieve the proficiencies. For many faculty members, this means taking more time and investing more effort than they may have initially thought necessary. It is important that you to modify your work now before moving on. To help guide your thinking in this area, we encourage you to refer to the learning experiences dimension of our course poster rubric (see Figure 7.3) before moving on. As always, you may also find it useful to ask a colleague to use the rubric to evaluate your work.

Using the Companion Website

The learning experiences (and the formative assessments in the following chapter) element of course design needs to be aligned with the proficiencies. If you are using the companion website, proficiencies added or deleted may affect the rest of the textboxes (which are automatically filled in); thus, you should return to the learning proficiencies chapter (Chapter 6) and edit the workboxes before moving forward to maintain the transparency and alignment of your learning pathway.

Of course, no matter how diligent you are in crafting learning experiences for your course, there is no guarantee of your students' success. As you lead your students along the path toward accomplishment of your

	Exceptional—No improvements needed	Good—Only minor improvements needed	Needs Work—Major improvements needed
LEARNING EXPERIENCES	Learning experiences are ***very likely to be sufficient*** in helping students develop the learning proficiencies. The approach taken is highly effective.	Learning experiences are ***probably sufficient*** to help students develop the learning proficiencies. Perhaps they could be supplemented by more or better experiences.	Learning experiences are ***likely to be insufficient*** to help students develop the learning proficiencies. Significant changes are likely to be needed.
Learning experiences are any experiences students have that help them learn the desired proficiencies, including in-class and experiences out-of-class experiences.	Use this space to write any comments/questions you have:		

FIGURE 7.3.   The Learning Experiences Dimension of Our Course Poster Rubric

learning goal, it will be important to build in checks to make sure that students are achieving the necessary proficiencies along the way. That is why formative assessment is a final critical element of our course design process; we turn to that in the next chapter.

Note

1. This point emphasizes Principle 7: learning doesn't depend on what is done to your students but instead on how they interpret their experiences. Lectures can serve an important role in helping students organize course material. However, done poorly, lectures reduce students to passive listeners and transcribers.

CHAPTER 8

Formative Assessment

Staying on Track

IN THIS FINAL CHAPTER of Part Two, we turn our attention to the last element of our course design process: formative assessment. In contrast to summative assessment (Chapter 5), which gathers information about your students' learning at the end of your course, formative assessment gathers information about student learning during your course. At first this difference in timing may appear relatively unimportant, but it has important implications for the purpose of the assessment activity (Palomba & Banta, 1999). As you saw in Chapter 5, the primary purpose of summative assessment is *evaluative*, allowing you to determine the extent to which you and your students were successful in reaching your final destination: your course goals. In contrast, the primary purpose of formative assessment is *improvement*; you'll be using formative assessment as your students move along the pathway to your goals to determine if they are staying on track. Using the language of our course design process, your focus will be examining the ways your learning experiences (Chapter 7) are successful in helping your students acquire the proficiencies (Chapter 6) they need to be successful. If students are indeed acquiring the needed proficiencies as you expect, then you can continue with your course's plan. On the other hand, if your students are not acquiring the necessary proficiencies, some sort of adjustment must be made by you and your students (e.g., additional practice, further concept development, exploration of more and different examples).[1]

Unfortunately, we've found that effective formative assessment is one of the most underappreciated practices in higher education, which leads us to Principle 9, shown in the following textbox. Too often faculty make assumptions about what their students are learning in their courses without any compelling evidence to support them. For instance, some faculty adopt an instruction-centered mind-set, falsely equating the quality of their own teaching performance with the quality of their students' learning. We see this when our colleagues say something akin to, "Students really learned a lot today. My presentation was very clear and well organized." It is only later, when students do poorly on an exam, final project, or written paper, that they discover the students aren't really getting it as they had originally thought. By that time it is too late for them (or their students, for that matter) to do anything to make needed adjustments (see Angelo & Cross, 1993, for a similar argument).

> Principle 9. Formative assessment allows you and your students to monitor progress along the pathway and make necessary adjustments to improve student learning.

We've also seen faculty try to focus on the quality of student learning in a way that does not take full advantage of the power of formative assessment. For instance, they may notice one or more students nodding approvingly during a classroom lecture, or they may notice that a particular student is asking especially insightful questions in class. In such cases, we've seen faculty use this information to infer that their students' learning is progressing as it should. However, they fail to recognize that the data they are basing that inference on are very limited, certainly too limited to be convincing. What these colleagues need, we insist, are more systematic ways to frequently gather evidence about the quality of their students' learning, including from students who are not nodding approvingly or asking insightful questions in class.[2] It is only then that more reasoned judgments can be made about where learning is really happening and where it needs to be improved.

The goal of this chapter is to help you integrate formative assessment into your course design. We begin by offering some ideas about how you can do this well. Later, we ask you to work through three distinct steps. First, in an exercise reminiscent of the one you performed in Chapter 7, you will brainstorm a list of possible formative assessment techniques for your course. Second, you will match one or more of those formative assessment techniques to each of the proficiencies you

identified in Chapter 6. Third, you will develop a specific plan for incorporating your formative assessment strategies into your course.

If done well, your work in this chapter will fit seamlessly with the other elements of your course design. In Chapter 6 you identified the proficiencies that are individually necessary and collectively sufficient for your students to achieve your learning goal. In Chapter 7 you created learning experiences for your students to develop those proficiencies. In this chapter, the focus is on determining the effectiveness of those learning experiences in developing the needed proficiencies. As a result, we ask you to identify one or more formative assessment tools for each and every proficiency you identified in Chapter 6. Your work in this chapter represents the final entries in your course poster (see Figure 8.1).

Throughout this chapter, we take you through the work you need to do by modeling the progression through a step-by-step process. We ask you to consider

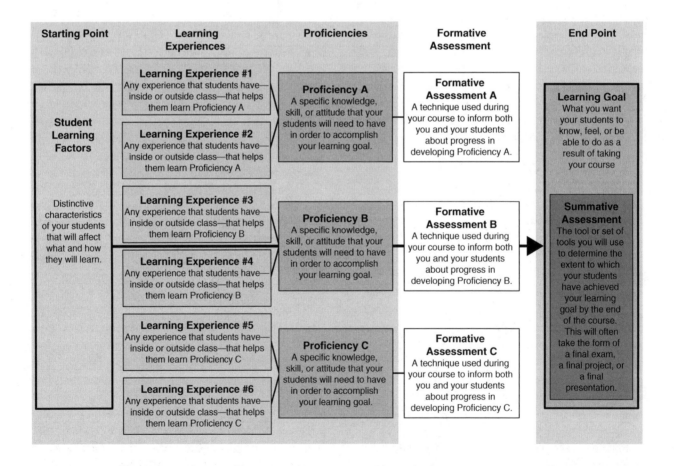

FIGURE 8.1. The Focus of This Chapter Is on Planning Formative Assessments for Your Selected Learning Goal (unshaded portion of the figure)

the example of an English professor teaching a course on Shakespearian literature. As one of her course goals (Chapter 5), she wanted her students to be able to analyze a variety of Shakespearian sonnets. In identifying the learning proficiencies (Chapter 6) needed to accomplish that goal, she noted that students had to be able to identify the structure of a Shakespearian sonnet, that is, 14 lines of iambic pentameter with a predictable rhyming scheme. To help students learn this proficiency, she planned to have students listen to a brief podcast of sonnets read out loud as well as listen to a mini lecture explaining the structure of sonnets. Her best judgment tells her these learning experiences (Chapter 7) should be sufficient to help her students achieve the desired proficiency. The professor is producing a plan for using formative assessment to inform her and her students about the degree of effectiveness of those learning experiences in developing the needed proficiency.

Sample Course on Shakespearean Literature

Learning goal: Analyze a variety of Shakespearian sonnets.

An early proficiency: Identify the structure of a Shakespearian sonnet.

Learning experiences designed to develop this proficiency:

- Students will listen to a podcast of sonnets being read out loud.
- Students will listen to a mini lecture explaining the structure of sonnets.

Characteristics of Effective Formative Assessment

Before moving directly to the step-by-step process of incorporating formative assessment into their courses, many faculty find it helpful to learn more about what they are striving for. As a result, in this section we outline four characteristics that make formative assessment particularly effective. As you build formative assessment techniques for your own course, we ask you to do so in a way that is consistent with the following four characteristics of formative assessment.

Characteristic 1: Makes Student Learning Visible

The most basic key to successful formative assessment is to make the learning of your students visible, as nearly all of what happens in the minds of your students is invisible. For you to gain access to your students' thinking, they have to do something that reveals what they are learning, such as completing some sort of work (e.g., small quizzes, homework assignments, etc.). Other times, this can be demonstrated when students are actively engaged in some sort of activity during class time (Angelo & Cross, 1993; Barkley, 2009). Regardless, the idea is for their learning to be visible so that you and your students can be better informed about the quality of their learning.

For example, consider how our English professor could assess whether students can successfully identify the structure of a Shakespearian sonnet. One approach would be to lead an in-class exercise in which she gives her students a collection of poems and asks students to identify which have the characteristics of Shakespearian sonnets and which do not. Further, students could be asked to identify what is missing in a poem that makes it inconsistent with the structure of a sonnet (e.g., it could have only 12 lines, a different meter, or a different pattern of rhyming). If students complete this exercise successfully, the professor would have evidence that students had acquired the desired proficiency. However, if students are unable to demonstrate proficiency in this exercise, then an additional learning experience may be needed. The key is that her students' learning is no longer hidden from view because the in-class exercise makes their learning visible.

Characteristic 2: Assesses the Learning of All Students

Effective formative assessment is also inclusive; that is, it collects information about the learning of all students, not just some. This is important because your obligation as a teacher is to promote the learning of all your students and not just those who are the most vocal or outspoken. Therefore, it is necessary to reveal the learning of everyone if possible.

Unfortunately, much of the formative assessment we see faculty members use in their classrooms is inconsistent with the notion of inclusiveness. For instance, many of our colleagues rely on some version of Socratic questioning characterized by frequent, targeted questioning of individual students. This method certainly makes for a lively classroom environment, and it can even be an effective way for the instructor to explore the levels of learning of individual students. However, it doesn't say anything at all about those students who remain silent. Are they learning as well? Unfortunately, it is impossible to know.

To be more inclusive, faculty members must find a way to reveal the learning of all their students. For instance, our Shakespearian literature professor could give the collection of poems to all her students and ask all of them to indicate whether each poem is a sonnet. This could be done in the form of a quiz or an assignment students complete for a grade. A less formal activity is also possible, such as asking students to vote on each poem by holding up a white sheet of paper if they think it is sonnet and a colored sheet of paper if they think it is not. Regardless, the activity should reveal the learning of all students.

Fortunately, technology is making it increasingly easy to administer these sorts of in-class assessments and to compile the results quickly. Rather than having students hold up sheets of colored paper, for instance, many faculty members rely on some form of student response system (i.e., clickers) consisting of a small device that allows students to answer questions posed during class time. One of the most significant benefits of this technology is that it is possible to compile a summary of students' responses in real time. Therefore, if students do have some fundamental misconception (e.g., about the structure of Shakespearian sonnets), it is very easy for the instructor to identify that misconception immediately. This increases the instructor's ability to react if he or she learns that students need additional help in a particular area.

Characteristic 3: Results Are Used for Improvement

Of course, merely administering a formative assessment tool and gathering information about your students' learning is not sufficient. The power of incorporating formative assessment into your course is using the results to improve student learning. For example, imagine that our English professor conducts her in-class exercise only to discover that her students perform poorly. It is not enough for her to merely take note of their poor performance and then move on to the next topic in her course. Instead, she should take

this opportunity to diagnose the specific area or areas students are having difficulty in and then provide the additional learning experiences necessary to improve. If the proficiency of describing the structure of a Shakespearian sonnet is necessary for students to succeed, then it would be foolhardy to do anything less.

Taking the results of your formative assessments seriously will almost certainly have implications for the flow or rhythm of your course. As a result, a certain amount of flexibility is required in your course design. When you outlined your sequence of learning experiences in Chapter 7, you did so on the basis of educated guesses about what students require to develop the desired proficiencies. If you have sufficient experience teaching your course, chances are good that your educated guesses are fairly accurate. However, in some cases you may have either overestimated or underestimated what students need to achieve your proficiencies. Using formative assessment can help you identify where your initial estimates are off. In those cases, your students will either develop the proficiencies more quickly and with less assistance than you thought would be necessary or more slowly and with more assistance than you anticipated. You can then make the necessary adjustments to better serve the learning needs of your students.

The need to make adjustments an the basis of how your students are progressing further highlights the importance of understanding your student learning factors. The more you can find out about the particular group of students in your course, the more informed your estimates will be about what learning experiences will be needed to accomplish the proficiencies in your course. Careful consideration of student learning factors will also reveal the diversity of your student population. Responding to the needs of a relatively heterogeneous group of students will obviously be more challenging than responding to the needs of a more homogeneous population. The following textbox presents one particularly challenging situation our faculty wrestle with in teaching their courses.

Characteristic 4: Gives Students Informative, Timely Feedback

Finally, it is worth noting that using formative assessment has benefits for more than just you, the instructor. An effective formative assessment can also serve as a valuable mechanism for providing feedback for your students. Hattie and Timperley (2007) define *feedback*

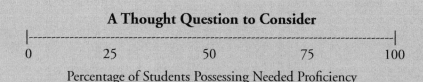

A Thought Question to Consider

Percentage of Students Possessing Needed Proficiency

If you administer a formative assessment in your course and 100% of your students demonstrate that they possess the proficiency needed to succeed, you should feel comfortable moving on to more complex material in your course.

In contrast, if you administer a formative assessment in your course and 0% of your students demonstrate that they possess the proficiency needed to succeed, you probably should not feel comfortable moving on to more complex material in your course.

What happens when the percentage of students demonstrating proficiency lies between 0 and 100%?

What do you see as your threshold for moving on in your course? That is, what percentage of your students would need to demonstrate that they possess a given proficiency to make you feel comfortable progressing to more complex material? If your answer is, "It depends," what are the factors it depends on?

as "information provided by an agent (e.g., teacher, peer, book, parent, self, experience) regarding one's performance or understanding" (p. 81). By making students' learning visible, formative assessment gives students feedback on that learning. They can see what they are doing well and what they are doing poorly and can be guided toward areas that may require additional time, effort, and study.

To achieve the maximum benefit from feedback opportunities, however, it is important for you to design your course in such a way that the students receive effective feedback to support their learning. For example, one of the key features of effective feedback is that it provides students with meaningful information about what they are doing correctly, what they are doing wrong, and what they can do to improve (Ambrose et al., 2010; Evans, 2013; Gibbs & Simpson, 2004; Hattie & Timperley, 2007). This sounds quite simple, but we have found that much of the feedback students receive is not sufficiently informative to help them improve their learning. For example, one of our STEM colleagues assigns his students a series of online homework problems at the end of each class period. The system he uses provides students with automated feedback about which questions they answer correctly and which ones they don't. However, when students answer incorrectly, the system merely indicates that they've done something wrong; it does nothing to inform students specifically

what they've done wrong or what they need to do to improve. As a result, his students learn more slowly than they might if the automated feedback were more informative.

Even when feedback on formative assessment tasks is not automated, one must be careful to ensure that feedback provides students with enough information to improve their learning. This is especially true if your formative assessments are in the form of graded assignments. If students receive only a C on a writing task or 75% on a set of homework problems, they don't really have sufficient information to guide their future learning. To be more useful, those grades should be accompanied by information that clearly shows the gap between their current level of performance and their ultimate performance destination (Evans, 2013; Hattie & Timperley, 2007).

An effective strategy for providing students with informative feedback is to evaluate their work using a grading rubric (Huba & Freed, 2000; Stevens & Levi, 2012).[3] In fact, if you plan to use a rubric to evaluate students' work on your summative assessment task, it is a good idea to introduce students to that rubric relatively early in the course and refer to it frequently as students are developing your proficiencies.[4] Doing so will help your students better understand the standards you will use to evaluate their success and can also show students where their current work stands relative to each of those standards.

Another important characteristic of effective feedback concerns timing. In general, feedback received quickly is more effective at guiding student learning than feedback that is delayed (Gibbs & Simpson, 2004). Prompt feedback allows students to take corrective actions while their original learning display is relatively fresh in their minds. For example, if students have to wait for an extended period for feedback on their work, they probably have moved on to other things by the time they get the feedback, which greatly reduces the benefits.

Gibbs and Simpson (2004) note the tension between these two characteristics of effective feedback. On the one hand, student learning is best supported if the feedback students receive is informative, guiding them toward what they need to do to improve. Providing students with that level of feedback often takes a significant amount of time, however, so they may not receive it very quickly. On the other hand, faculty aiming to provide quicker feedback, such as our STEM colleague using the automated approach, may end up providing feedback that lacks a sufficient level of information to be maximally helpful.

We see our very best faculty colleagues wrestling with this tension on a daily basis. While there are no simple ways to resolve this tension, there are three approaches many of our colleagues use successfully. First, many faculty report success in creating formative assessment tasks that are not graded or at least not all graded. Part of the struggle faculty members face in reviewing student work is in assigning grades, which isn't necessary to provide students with feedback about their progress. In fact, Black and Wiliam (1998) suggest that students may benefit more from feedback that is not accompanied by a grade, simply because students who receive grades are so preoccupied with their grades that the information value of other feedback may be overlooked.

Another strategy used by many of our colleagues is to provide feedback in the aggregate rather than at the individual level. Several of our colleagues ask students to display some aspect of their learning and then turn in that display, often in written form, at the end of a class period. Before the next class, the professor reviews what students submitted and then summarizes the overall strengths and weaknesses at the beginning of the following class. This aggregated feedback may not be as richly informative as specific feedback for

each individual student, but the disadvantage of presenting it in aggregate is offset by the timeliness in providing the feedback.

Finally, feedback does not necessarily need to come from you for it to be effective. Given the right conditions, students are able to give meaningful feedback to each other. They could be asked to review one another's writing assignments with an eye toward identifying thesis statements, topic sentences, particularly clear or confusing arguments, and so on (Nilson, 2003). By using a peer feedback approach, students receive the benefits of informative feedback, and because the workload associated with reviewing the writing assignments is distributed across multiple students, they receive that feedback relatively quickly.[5]

With these strategies in mind, let's return to the example of our Shakespearian literature professor. In an effort to provide informative, timely feedback to her students, she may ask them to turn in written responses at the end of a class period in the form of an ungraded quiz. Before the next class, she reviews students' responses to determine which attributes of the sonnets students seem to understand and which ones they don't. At the beginning of the next class session, she points out those areas and follows up with supplementary instruction if needed. Providing students with information about what they can do to improve, and doing so in a timely manner, gives her students the best chance to learn the structure of a Shakespearian sonnet.

Summary: Characteristics of Effective Formative Assessment

1. Effective formative assessment makes learning visible.
2. Effective formative assessment is inclusive, collecting information from all students.
3. The results of effective formative assessment are used to improve learning.
4. Effective formative assessment allows students to receive informative, timely feedback.

Step 1: Brainstorm Possible Formative Assessment Techniques

In this chapter we ask you to brainstorm a list of formative assessment techniques. We suggest you refer to Angelo and Cross's (1993) landmark book, *Classroom Assessment Techniques*, as well as any of several other excellent collections of teaching tips (e.g., Davis, 2009; Svinicki & McKeachie, 2013). Table 8.1 contains some possible examples.

TABLE 8.1: Step 1: Examples of Possible Formative Assessment Techniques

Name of technique	How does this technique make learning visible?	Example of how technique is put into action	Reference for more information
Just-in-time teaching	Prior to a lesson, students respond to an open-ended question related to the topic and submit their answers to an online server.	Before a biology lesson on cloning, students complete the assigned reading and then answer a series of questions related to the topic (e.g., Dolly is a clone of a sheep born six years earlier. Does Dolly have parents? Why or why not?). Review students' answers before the lesson and weave students' responses into the day's activities.	Novak & Patterson (2010)
Minute paper	Students write a short response to a question posed at the end of a class session.	At the end of an introductory lesson on the civil war, students summarize what they've learned during that day's class. After class, read students' responses to determine if they have picked up on the most important points.	Angelo & Cross (1993)
Student response systems (i.e., clickers)	During a class session, students answer a question using an electronic student response system.	In a class on constitutional law, students often get confused about the scope of the Bill of Rights. Halfway through the lesson, students answer a clicker question. The software automatically compiles a frequency distribution of student responses, which shows the percentage of the class that is following and the percentage that isn't.	Duncan (2005)
Ungraded quiz	Following a lecture or other learning experience, students are asked to complete a quiz on the course material. While not submitted for a grade, the quiz is still useful as a way to check students' learning.	In a class on Shakespearean literature, give students a series of poems. Using what they know about the structure of sonnets, students identify which are sonnets and which are not.	Bonwell (1996)

Using the entries in the example in Table 8.1 as your guide, we ask you to think of additional formative assessment techniques, which can be anything students do to make their learning visible, either in class (the ungraded quiz used in the Shakespearian literature class) or outside class (in the preclass work in just-in-time teaching), and write them down in Workbox 8.1. Be aware that some of the best formative assessment techniques are natural outgrowths of the learning experiences you have already generated. For instance, the Shakespearian literature professor may give students the categorization task to help them learn the distinction between sonnets and other poems. While this task may be a valuable learning experience in its own right, by being attentive to the level of student performance on the task, the instructor can also use the task as a valuable source of formative assessment. Similarly, we encourage you to consult the list of learning experiences you generated in Chapter 7 to see if you can also use them to collect information about the status of your students' learning.

Step 2: Match Formative Assessment Techniques to Proficiencies

Once you have brainstormed a list of formative assessment techniques, narrow your list by choosing the techniques that are the most appropriate for each of the proficiencies you identified in Chapter 6. This is similar to the work you did in Chapter 7, when you matched learning experiences to proficiencies. By ensuring at least one formative assessment technique matches each and every one of your proficiencies, you can be sure that your design reaps the benefits of formative assessment at each step of your course. The example in Table 8.2 shows how the Shakespearian literature professor would complete this step.

WORKBOX 8.1.
Brainstorming Formative Assessment Techniques

Name of technique	How learning is made visible	Example of how I would put this technique into action in my course

TABLE 8.2: Step 2: An Example of Matching a Formative Assessment Technique to a Proficiencies

Example learning goal: Analyze a variety of Shakespearian sonnets

Proficiency	Learning experience	Formative assessment technique
Describe the structure of a Shakespearian sonnet	Students listen to a podcast of sonnets read out loud. Students listen to a mini lecture explaining the structure of sonnets.	Ungraded quiz. Show students a series of poems and ask them whether each one is written in the structure of a sonnet. Ask them to describe what is missing in the poems that are not sonnets.

WORKBOX 8.2.
Match Formative Assessment Techniques to Proficiencies

Learning goal:

Proficiency	Learning experience	Formative assessment technique

Given the myriad formative assessment techniques that are possible, the one that is the most appropriate for each of your proficiencies may not be the most obvious. To repeat, the purpose of formative assessment is to provide you and your students with good information about their development of the proficiencies. Many formative assessment techniques are natural outgrowths of the learning experiences you have already paired with each proficiency. For instance, the in-class exercise used by the professor of Shakespearian literature could easily be scheduled immediately after the mini lecture that she is already planning to give in class.

Any formative assessment technique you choose will also need to fit into the practical considerations of your course or institution. While it might be ideal to regularly provide one-on-one verbal feedback to each of the students in your course, it may be impossible if you have more than just a few students. Therefore, only the formative assessment techniques that can realistically be incorporated into your course should go in Workbox 8.2.

As with all elements of your course design, we encourage you to discuss your choices in Workbox 8.2 with your peers. At our course design retreat, these discussions take place in face-to-face meetings between faculty members. We urge users of this book to seek out similar interactions in meetings with peers, friends, or trusted colleagues on their home campuses.

Step 3: Incorporate Formative Assessment Into Your Course

Once you have identified appropriate formative assessment techniques and matched them with their corresponding proficiencies, it is time to incorporate them into the flow of your course. Specifically, your task is to plan your use of each technique so that you are proceeding in a way that is consistent with the characteristics of effective formative assessment. For each of your chosen techniques, you will need to be able to answer the following questions:

- How does this technique make student learning visible?
- Is this technique inclusive?
- How will you use the results of the formative assessment to improve student learning?
- How will students receive informative, timely feedback?

The example in Table 8.3 shows how our Shakespearian literature professor would answer each of these questions for her course.

For each the formative assessment techniques you identified in Workbox 8.2, follow the example of our Shakespearian literature professor and write your answers to these questions in Workbox 8.3, the culminating workbox for this chapter. Your responses are the final piece of your course poster.

TABLE 8.3: Step 3: Incorporate Formative Assessment Into Your Course

Example learning goal: Analyze a variety of Shakespearian sonnets

Proficiency	Formative assessment techniques	How does this technique make learning visible?	Is this technique inclusive?	How will you use the results of the formative assessment?	How will students receive informative, timely feedback?
Describe the structure of a Shakespearian sonnet	Ungraded quiz. I will show students a series of poems and ask them to identify whether each one is written in the structure of a sonnet. For those that are not, I will ask them to describe what is missing.	For each poem, students will write their responses on a sheet of paper, which they will turn in at the end of class.	Yes. All students will be asked to turn in their written responses.	I will examine the pattern of right and wrong answers for any meaningful patterns. During the next class period, I will review those areas in which students had difficulties.	I will debrief each of the correct answers in class following the exercise. Students will also receive personalized feedback on their written submission.

WORKBOX 8.3.
Incorporate Formative Assessment Into Your Course

Learning goal:

Proficiency	Formative assessment technique	How does this technique make learning visible?	Is this technique inclusive?	How will you use the results of the formative assessment?	How will students receive informative, timely feedback?
A.	A.				
B.	B.				
C.	C.				
D.	D.				

	Exceptional—No improvements needed	Good—Only minor improvements needed	Needs Work—Major improvements needed
FORMATIVE ASSESSMENT	Formative assessment provides you and your students with *meaningful information* about students' acquisition of learning proficiencies, including information about what you or they need to do to improve.	Formative assessment provides you and your students with *some information* about students' acquisition of learning proficiencies. However, data are incomplete and may not provide sufficient information about what you or they need to do to improve.	Formative assessments are either missing or provide *inadequate information* about students' acquisition of learning proficiencies.
Formative assessment is the gathering of information about student learning in a way that can be used to improve the quality of that learning. This is the assessment performed during the course rather than at the end.	Use this space to write any comments/questions you have:		

FIGURE 8.2. The Formative Assessment Dimension of Our Course Poster Rubric

To evaluate your work in this chapter, we encourage you to use the formative assessment dimension of our course poster rubric, shown in Figure 8.2. You may also wish to ask a colleague to use the rubric to evaluate your work.

Notes

1. In our experience, many faculty assume that students are the only ones who need to adjust what they are doing in the face of poor performance on a formative assessment. Often, that comes in the form of asking (or telling) the students to work harder or study more. Working harder or studying more can be interpreted by students as merely spending more time with the material. By itself, this may or may not be an effective strategy to improve student learning (Treisman, 1992).

2. At our course design retreat, some of our own faculty colleagues bristle at the notion of such frequent use of formative assessment. Their most significant concern is time; they don't realize that they have enough time to check in with their students for each and every one of the proficiencies in their course. Furthermore, they claim that any time spent engaging in formative assessment takes away from time that could be spent moving on to more complex material. In response, we say that while engaging in formative assessment does take at least some time, the benefits easily justify the time investment required. In fact, we've found that regularly performing formative assessment saves a lot of headaches in the long run, simply because it will help you and your students identify shortcomings while there is still enough time to make improvements. Furthermore, many of the formative assessment techniques that can provide rich information about your students' learning can be done relatively quickly and are surprisingly easy to incorporate into your course.

3. For assistance in creating a grading rubric for your course assignments, see Stevens & Levi (2012), which provides step-by-step guidance on how to construct effective rubrics.

4. In the name of transparency, note that we have tried to follow our own advice in this book. Although we include the entire rubric we use to evaluate faculty members' course posters in Appendix A, we have provided relevant dimensions of the rubric throughout the book so you can evaluate your own work as you progress. This allows you to assess your work as you construct each element of your course design and make adjustments as needed. Ultimately, this will lead you to a more effective final product.

5. Sometimes students will need guidance from you on how to effectively offer feedback so that it is not about how they feel but rather that they are applying the appropriate criteria.

PART THREE

Pulling the Elements Together

CHAPTER 9

The Course Poster

Visualizing the Pathway for Student Learning

CONGRATULATIONS ON FULLY CONSTRUCTING the complete pathway for one of your course goals! In this chapter, your task is to pull together all the course design pieces you've worked on up to this point and incorporate them into a visual display, which we call the course design poster, using the format shown in Figure 9.1. Creating this poster on paper or online will help you (and others) see the logic behind the course you have worked so hard to design.

At our course design retreat, our faculty participants create posters similar to the one shown in Figure 9.1, and we dedicate several hours on the last day of the retreat to allow participants to present their posters to one another in a conference-style setting. Although we cannot physically re-create that poster session here, we ask you to create a poster for your course and share it with your peers, colleagues, or friends on your home campus. Doing so can be very helpful as you review the work you've done and begin thinking about the implementation of your course design.

In our work with faculty members, we have discovered at least three significant benefits associated with developing a course poster and sharing it with others. First, creating a course poster can be a deeply reflective exercise for course designers. By progressing to this point in the course design process, you have completed a lot of difficult work, and now is a terrific time to sit back and celebrate your progress. We have also found that participating in this process helps course designers clarify their thinking. In general, faculty members are not in the habit of showing their course design visually and then presenting it to colleagues and students. To make these presentations understandable, concise, and logical, faculty members need to be crystal clear about the function and role of each element of their course design and how the different elements interact with one another. Deep clarity of thought will allow you to clearly describe the details of your course design to others.

A second benefit of creating a course poster and presenting it to others is that it allows your peers to review your work, which can further guide your thinking. Remember that the course design process is most effective if it is interactive and iterative, and we've intentionally designed the process so that you frequently have a chance to present your ideas, get feedback from your peers, and then refine your thinking accordingly. Creating and presenting this visual display is just the next step in the process.

Third, we have found that the course poster can be a potentially powerful way for you to communicate the details of your course design to your students. All too often, faculty members teach courses without making any overt attempt to share the logic of their course design with their students. As a result, students are often unsure why they are taking particular courses, what those courses are supposed to help them do, or why a course's assignments or tests are set up the way they are. To combat this, we urge you to share the thinking that went into your course design with your students, perhaps in the syllabus (see Chapter 10) or during one of the early lessons of the course. Regardless, we have found that students respond positively if they know and understand the whys of your course and if they can see a clear pathway to success (Principle 10).

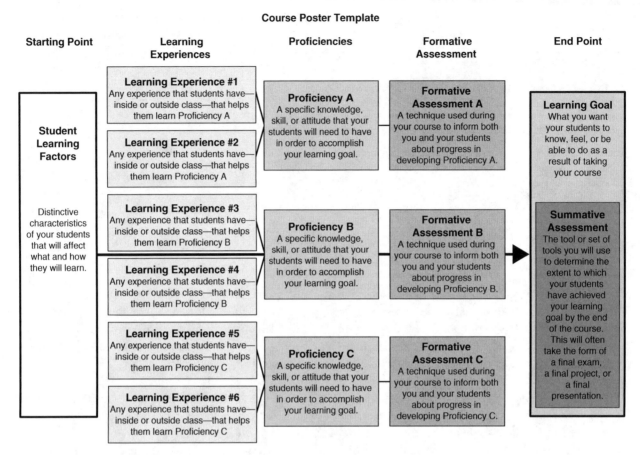

FIGURE 9.1.   Overview of the Course Design Process as Shown by a Template for Your Course Poster

Principle 10. An effective pathway is clear to all.

To achieve the benefits of creating and presenting a course poster, we ask you to communicate and review the details of your course design. You will need to be attentive to how you represent each of the course design elements you've worked on up until now, and you will also need to pay attention to how you represent the relationships between each of those elements. If successful, by the time you reach the end of the chapter, you will have created at least one highly effective poster for your course.[1]

Throughout the book, we have referred to a rubric that we use to evaluate the course posters created by our own faculty colleagues. That rubric, presented in its entirety in Appendix A, includes separate rows for each element of the course design you worked on in

Chapters 3–8 and contains rows for the global characteristics of transparency, alignment, and integration, which we introduced in Chapter 1. We encourage you to use this rubric in reviewing your own work or the work of your peers.

Step 1: Create a Draft of Your Poster

Your first step is to create a visual display of the work you've done thus far with a single course goal. At our course design retreat, we typically have participants display their course designs in Microsoft PowerPoint, placing all the design elements on a single slide. PowerPoint is a useful application because nearly all our colleagues already know how to use it, and when connected to a digital projector, the software makes it easy for users to display their poster for everyone to see. If you are familiar with an alternative application (e.g., Keynote, Prezi) that you think is more suitable for creating your course design poster, you may certainly use that instead.

The easiest way to create your poster is to draw on the work you have done in the previous chapters. To simplify this process, the companion website (https://styluspub.presswarehouse.com/products/buildingapathway.aspx) takes your responses to the culminating workboxes in Chapters 3–8 and automatically creates a draft poster, as shown in Figure 9.2.

Step 2: Review Each Course Design Element

Once you've created a rough draft of your poster, review each of the course design elements you generated in Chapters 3–8. While you already dedicated significant time and energy to these elements when you were working through the earlier chapters, it may have been a while since you reviewed each of them. Many faculty members find it helpful to review their thoughts on each element once they have made it all the way through the course design process; this is yet another example of the iterative nature of the design process.

Table 9.1 contains some of the most important questions you should answer as you reflect on the work you have done so far. These same questions serve as the basis for the evaluation rubric in Appendix A.

Step 3: Check for Transparency

Once you have reviewed each element of your course design, examine your poster as a whole. The first and simplest characteristic to look for is transparency (see Appendix A), which means that the design is clear to everyone, including you, your colleagues, and your students. Anyone viewing your poster should able to understand your course design with minimal additional explanation from you.

The best way to gauge the transparency of your course design is to show your poster to someone not directly connected to your course. In fact, at our course design retreat, we have participants show their posters to colleagues from different disciplines. This helps course designers overcome the "curse of knowledge" (Heath & Heath, 2007, p. 20) because it forces them

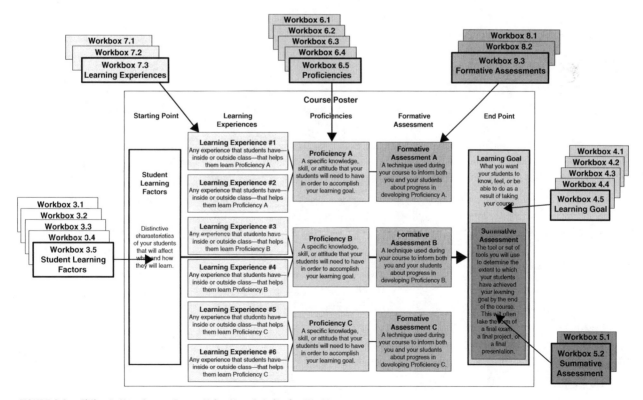

FIGURE 9.2. Filling In Your Course Poster Using Your Culminating Workboxes

TABLE 9.1: Questions to Ask Yourself as You Review Each Element of Your Course Design

Course Design Element	*Chapter*	*Questions You Need to Be Able to Answer*
Student learning factors	3	• What are the most significant student learning factors in your course? • How will those student learning factors affect student learning in your course? • Have you considered ○ the distinctive characteristics of students at your institution? ○ where your students are situated in your institution? ○ your students' prior experiences? ○ the knowledge, skills, and attitudes your students are likely to possess?
Learning goals	4	• How well does your goal operationalize the dream you have for student learning? • Have you written your goal so that it meets the criteria for ○ clarity? ○ focusing on student performance? ○ requiring high levels of thinking that are developmentally appropriate? ○ connecting all aspects of the course? ○ being worthwhile and significant?
Summative assessment	5	• Is your summative assessment aligned with your learning goal? That is, are the actions students need to take to be successful on your summative assessment the same as the actions needed to demonstrate the accomplishment of your learning goal? • Is your summative assessment authentic? • Will your summative assessment yield a product and the thought process that led to it?
Learning proficiencies	6	• What knowledge, skills, and attitudes must students have to accomplish your stated course goal? • Are the proficiencies on your list individually necessary and collectively sufficient? • Have you sequenced the proficiencies in a way that is logical?
Learning experiences	7	• Have you identified one or more learning experiences for each of your proficiencies? • Are those learning experiences ○ aligned? ○ engaging? ○ well supported? ○ efficient? • Taken together, are the learning experiences sufficient to accomplish your stated proficiencies?

(Continues)

TABLE 9.1: Questions to Ask Yourself as You Review Each Element of Your Course Design (Continued)

Course Design Element	Chapter	Questions You Need to Be Able to Answer
Formative assessment	8	• Have you identified at least one formative assessment mechanism for each of your proficiencies? • How does each technique make student learning visible? • Is each technique inclusive? • How will you use the results of the formative assessment to improve student learning? • How will students receive informative, timely feedback about the quality of their learning?

to state the details of their course design so clearly that even someone who lacks their disciplinary expertise can understand them.

Step 4: Check for Alignment

The next characteristic to check for is alignment (see Appendix A). Overall, your course is aligned when all the course elements point you and your students in the same direction—toward the desired learning goal.

In our experience, poor alignment is a very common problem in college course design. Students often encounter courses that either lack well-articulated learning goals or have poorly aligned assessments, proficiencies, or learning experiences. This misalignment puts students in a tenuous and frustrating position. For instance, they may work hard to develop a course's stated proficiencies only to face a summative assessment focused on something else.[2] Misalignment muddles the pathway to student success, while a better aligned course makes it much clearer.

Because alignment is so important, it is a pervasive theme throughout the design process. In Chapter 5 we asked you to ensure that your summative assessment is aligned with your goal, in Chapter 6 we asked you to create learning proficiencies that align with your summative assessment, and in Chapters 7 and 8 we asked that the learning experiences and formative assessments align with your proficiencies. It is still helpful to take the time to double-check to ensure that all the elements are correctly aligned throughout your course.

To illustrate the importance of performing an overall alignment check, consider the following analogy.

Imagine a carpenter who is attempting to use a 12-inch ruler to draw a straight line across an 8-foot-wide piece of plywood. Because the ruler is much smaller than the overall width of the board, the carpenter will be forced to draw multiple shorter lines across the board. Using the ruler will make it relatively easy for the carpenter to ensure that each of his 12-inch segments is straight. However, it may be much more difficult for him to ensure that the 12-inch segment on the far left side of the board is on a straight line with the 12-inch segment on the far right side of the board. In other words, drawing a series of straight 12-inch lines may not guarantee that the resulting line is straight across the entirety of the 8-foot-piece of wood.

Applying this analogy to course design, consider the course poster in Figure 9.3, which is an example of what a professor of plant biology (see Chapter 7) might produce after working through each of the elements of the course design process. Overall, this poster is a relatively good first draft; however, the alignment across the entire poster is less than perfect. Further examination of the poster shows that even the smallest misalignment between the individual elements can add up to a significant misalignment overall.

Take a close look at Figure 9.3, and see if you can identify specific places where overall alignment could be improved. What improvements would you recommend? The following are some of our observations about this poster.

Misalignment of student learning factors with other course elements. The student learning factors make it clear that students are unfamiliar with how to use a field guide. Yet, we see nothing in the learning experiences, or other elements of the course design, that

Plant Biology

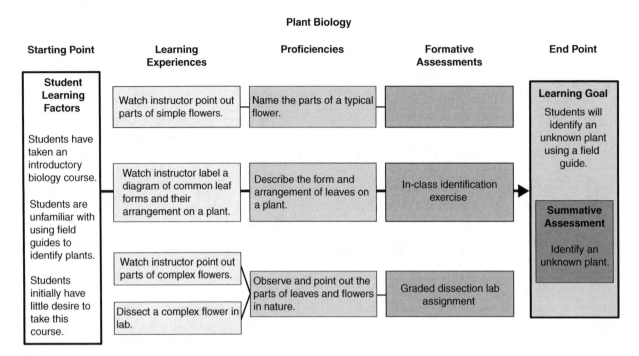

FIGURE 9.3.　Example of a Poorly Aligned Course Design

will help them learn how to use a field guide. Students would be unlikely to make their way successfully to the learning goal without some additional guidance and practice.

Misalignment of learning goals and summative assessment. While the summative assessment (Identify an unknown plant) is similar to the learning goal (Students will identify an unknown plant using a field guide), they are not identical. Most notably, the summative assessment says nothing about using a field guide. Because of this omission, none of the proficiencies, learning experiences, or formative assessments have anything to do with using a field guide, which students don't already know how to use. This seemingly minor omission could have important long-term implications for the overall success of the course. Therefore, we recommend modifying the wording of the summative assessment to more closely align with the ultimate course goal, which would then have a cascading effect on the other course design elements in the poster.

Misalignment between proficiencies and the goal. While the proficiencies in this poster are certainly necessary for student success, they are all focused on relatively low-level skills associated with identifying the different parts of plants. Even if students were to

achieve these proficiencies, we would not be confident they would be able to succeed on the more complex summative assessment of identifying unfamiliar plants. We recommend that this professor display proficiencies from the broader course, perhaps one each from the early, middle, and later periods in the students' developmental pathway, to better represent the range of proficiencies students will ultimately need to acquire.

Misalignment between learning experiences and proficiencies. We are concerned with the relatively passive nature of many of the learning experiences listed on the poster. Three of the four learning experiences involve nothing more than watching the instructor do something, such as point out the parts of simple flowers, which may not be the most effective way to promote learning the stated proficiencies. If the learning goal is to have students identify plants, we recommend that students take on a more active role in learning the relevant proficiencies.

Misalignment between proficiencies and formative assessment. Finally, notice that no formative assessment mechanism is identified for the first proficiency: Name the parts of a typical flower. This is troublesome, particularly because this proficiency is so foundational. Students would likely be lost if the course proceeded

Plant Biology

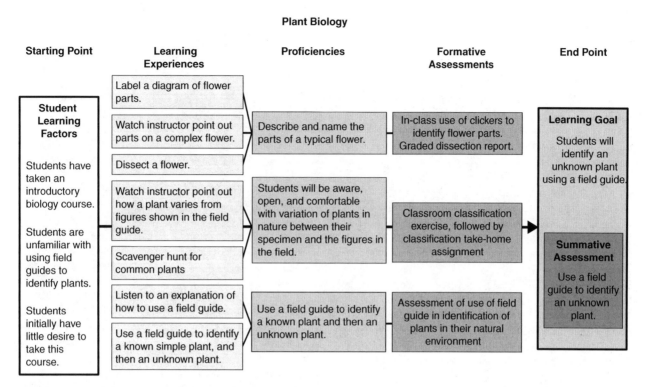

FIGURE 9.4.   Example of a Well-Aligned Course Design

without them being able to master it. We recommend that the course designer build in some kind of mechanism to ensure that students have indeed acquired this foundational principle before moving on to more complex proficiencies.

Each of the observations we made about Figure 9.3 are relatively easy to address. Figure 9.4 shows a revised poster from the same botany professor, which is a much stronger product, as it addresses each of our concerns:

- The student learning factors (unfamiliarity with field guides and low motivation) are now directly addressed in the proficiencies and learning experiences.
- The summative assessment has been revised to more closely match the stated learning goal.
- The proficiencies now reflect the broader course, including the more complex skill of using a plant guide to identify plants.
- The learning experiences include some instructor-led experiences, but they also include an array of more engaged activities for students to learn the stated proficiencies.

- There are now formative assessments for each of the proficiencies. Furthermore, it is relatively easy to see how each of these assessments make learning visible, are inclusive, and can provide feedback to students. Our only remaining question is how the faculty member plans to use the results of those formative assessments to inform the direction of his course.

Step 5: Revisit Your Other Course Goals, Look for Points of Integration

Up to this point in the course design process, we have asked you to elaborate on only one of your course goals because we have generally found that faculty members have an easier time working through the various stages of the course design process if they focus their energy on only one goal at a time. However, we are also aware that most course designers are interested in students accomplishing several different learning goals in their course. Therefore, to develop a more complete design of your course, repeat the process for each of your other course goals. We encourage you to refer to

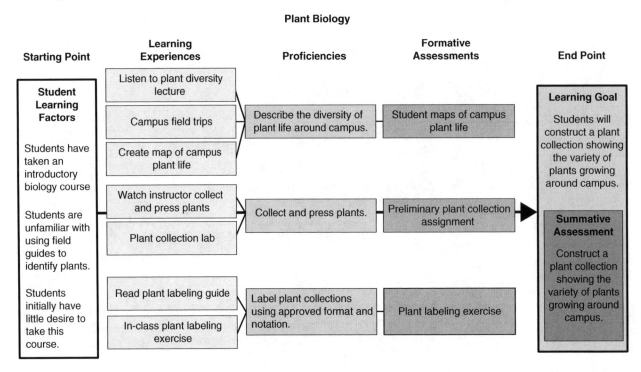

FIGURE 9.5. Sample Poster for a Second Course Goal in a Plant Biology Course

the workboxes in Chapters 5–8 for each of the goals you articulated in Chapter 4, ultimately resulting in a separate course poster for each of your goals.

Each course poster you create should meet the standards we have set for transparency and alignment. In addition, we call for a final characteristic: integration (see Appendix A). In a well-integrated course the different course goals work together, perhaps by jointly contributing to a common summative assessment. In contrast, a course that is not well integrated has course goals that are independent of one another. In short, a well-integrated course requires students to connect learning goals through its summative assessments, proficiencies, and learning experiences; a poorly integrated course allows students to accomplish the learning goals separately without drawing connections between them.

We ask you to look for possible areas of integration across the multiple learning goals of your course. Fortunately, these opportunities are relatively easy to see when you look at multiple posters from the same course. For example, let's return to the example from our botany professor. Upon finalizing the poster for his first course goal (see Figure 9.4), this professor

proceeded to create a similar poster for his second course goal: Construct a plant collection showing the variety of plants growing around campus. That second poster is shown in Figure 9.5.

Our botany professor's first course goal, shown in Figure 9.4 (Students will identify an unknown plant using a field guide), is clearly distinct from the second course goal, shown in Figure 9.5 (Students will construct a plant collection showing the variety of plants growing around campus). However, these two course goals could work together. For instance, a common summative assessment could be used to provide information on both course goals. That is, students could be asked to collect a variety of plants from around campus, identifying each one, even those they are initially unfamiliar with, using a field guide. Their final grade on this project could be a reflection of their plant identification skills and their skills in constructing the final plant collection.[3]

Another point of possible integration comes from the campus field trips mentioned in the learning experiences section of the poster in Figure 9.5. Campus field trips are shown only in the second course goal poster (Figure 9.5), tied to the proficiency of describing the diversity of plant life around campus. However, these trips could serve multiple purposes: They could also be used to help students learn to use a field guide, a key proficiency from the first course goal poster (Figure 9.4). By having specific course experiences that serve multiple course goals, students will have a more integrated course experience.

Using the Companion Website

As a resource and as a reminder, the companion website (https://styluspub.presswarehouse.com/products/buildingapathway.aspx) automatically generates the course poster based upon what you have filled into the final workboxes (or components of those workboxes) in the previous chapters. Figure 9.2 illustrates which workboxes populate the respective parts of the course poster. This resource may be especially useful as you consider additional course goals or other courses.

Conclusion

In this chapter we ask you to generate a course poster for at least one of your course goals. As you create additional posters for your other course goals, we encourage you to share them with your peers, colleagues, and friends to maximize the chances that the various elements of your course are sound and well aligned. By producing separate posters for each of your other course goals, you will also be able to determine if your different course goals work together in a well-integrated way. We are confident that if you do this, you will be well on your way to a highly successful course.

Notes

1. As you will ultimately be creating separate course posters for each of the course goals you identified in Chapter 4, you can use this chapter as an opportunity to create multiple posters, one for each of your course goals.
2. In our faculty development workshops, we typically ask our colleagues if they have ever taken a course in which they were on the receiving end of this type of poor alignment. We've yet to encounter someone who didn't have at least one frustrating experience of this sort.
3. For the purposes of record keeping, it would be especially useful if students received separate grades for each course goal, even if they were each assigned following a common summative assessment. This would allow the professor to summarize students' performance on each goal separately, which would be especially helpful for assessment and accreditation purposes as well as for improving the course in the future.

CHAPTER 10

The Course Syllabus

Students' Pathway to Success

IT'S THE FIRST DAY of the semester, and students anxiously await meeting you and the other students, and learning about the course. They probably ask themselves, *Who is the instructor? What kind of experience will this be? Will the classroom atmosphere be cool or warm? What kind of workload will the course demand? What will be expected of us?* Some students enter your course with confidence, whereas others may enter with doubts about their ability to succeed. But in all cases, their first encounter with your course and the answers to some of their questions are in your course syllabus.

Many faculty view the syllabus as solely an administrative document. While it certainly has an administrative component to it, an effective syllabus goes further and capitalizes on its power to propel the course forward and create the course's identity and personality. An effective learning-centered syllabus reveals your course design to students in a way that makes sense to them, in a form that gives them a snapshot of the whole course. It emphasizes what students will be learning in the course rather than what will be delivered.

The syllabus is a different communication vehicle from the poster you created in Chapter 9. The poster is part of the design process that allows you to put some distance between you and your work, step back, and show it to others to help you assess its transparency and alignment. The syllabus, on the other hand, is one of the products of your design and is the tool, or vehicle, students use to put themselves on the learning pathway.

As the primary means to communicate your design, your syllabus addresses students' questions about the journey they are about to embark on. From a learner's perspective, what do they need to know to start off on the right foot? From your perspective, what do you want to communicate? What do you want to emphasize? What impressions do you want to make?

This chapter helps you answer these questions and build the mental framework necessary to make decisions about the learning-centered syllabus you want to create. (For an example of a learning-centered syllabus, see Appendix C.) You will be incorporating the six elements of course design (i.e., student factors, goals, summative assessment, formative assessment, proficiencies, and learning experiences) into an effective syllabus. Your syllabus can take on many forms, but to be effective, it must clearly communicate (a) a positive attitude about the course through its tone as well as motivate the students to care and learn; (b) the learning goals of the course, or what students will accomplish by taking the course; (c) what students need to do to be successful and how the course will help students achieve the course goals; and (d) the necessary administrative information. (Administrative information is an essential part of any syllabus, but we have chosen to address it last because it is the part of the syllabus that is least related to your design for student learning.) Each of these ideas is described in more detail in the sections that follow.

Step 1: Describe the Impressions You Want Your Course Syllabus to Make

Your syllabus is a powerful communication tool for establishing a positive learning environment from the moment the course commences on day one. The tone of your syllabus, along with its presentation, is the overarching characteristic you have to get right because the tone communicates your attitude toward the subject and toward the students (Ambrose et al., 2010). You establish the tone of your syllabus through your words, language, and punctuation. The syllabus is the very first thing students see, feel, and use to rapidly form an impression of you, your competence, and your course. Research has shown that students form impressions within the first two hours of the course, and those impressions persist all the way to the end of the course months later (Kohlan, 1973). In other words, students form impressions within the first two class periods that stay virtually unchanged throughout the semester. Student first impressions influence their judgments about an instructor's approachability (Ishiyama & Hartlaub, 2002); their subsequent behaviors, such as engagement (Bond, 1972); and incivilities, such as tardiness and inappropriate cell phone use (Boice, 1998). Therefore, your syllabus represents an opportunity to motivate and inspire students to adjust their behaviors and put in the energy necesary to learn.

As an example, suppose a student enters a chemistry course with a neutral attitude. How will that attitude shift after reading the first few lines of the syllabus from a required organic chemistry course shown in the following textbox? What are the student's first impressions likely to be? What words describe the syllabus's tone? What kind of attitude does it convey? Is the instructor perceived as a partner or an adversary? What kind of learning environment does it create?

Attitude and First Impressions

Welcome to Chem 250!!

This course is designed to teach you some organic chemistry, and that alone may be somewhat daunting. You may have heard the horror stories of organic chemistry being the bane of any science student's existence—mostly that's true.

In Workbox 10.1 list words that describe how you want your course to be perceived, such as *challenging, fun, worthwhile, tough, insightful, useful,* or *transformative.*

Now that you have a list of words for your syllabus, use language consistent with these words. In the chemistry example, words and phrases like *daunting* (i.e., tending to overwhelm or intimidate), *horror stories*, and *bane of existence* (i.e., a cause of harm, ruin, death, or a source of persistent annoyance or exasperation) all evoke strong negative reactions from students. In a required course like organic chemistry, students may feel trapped and threatened reading such language in the syllabus, possibly provoking the stressful fight-or-flight response.

It is also important to avoid phrasing that sends a message to students that you expect them to exhibit negative behavior. We've read numerous syllabi that

WORKBOX 10.1.
Creating a Positive Impression

In this workbox, list words that describe how you want your course to be perceived through your syllabus. What impressions do you want students to have after reading your syllabus?

include long lists of rules about what students should not do (e.g., Don't turn in work that is not your own.). While you may wish to use the syllabus to establish course policies, we've found that students respond more favorably to expectations that are phrased positively (e.g., We value academic integrity in this class.). Otherwise, you risk turning off students who are sincere, hardworking, courteous, and ethical—the very students you are trying to motivate.

On the other hand, we are not advocating for you to sugarcoat or downplay the challenges ahead. After all, you want your course to induce students to think, feel, and act in ways that may feel uncomfortable. Thinking is hard work, uncertain, and avoided by many people (Willingham, 2009). Courses that have difficult, abstract, and complex concepts, such as organic chemistry, demand a deep level of commitment and hard work from students. Motivating students to achieve this high level of performance and success demands a very positive tone and attitude in the learning environment.

Another powerful way your syllabus can present a positive attitude and spirit is through its visual design. Many course syllabi we have reviewed have a dull, unexciting, administrative appearance that does not motivate students to read them or even refer to them. As advertisers and marketing professionals clearly understand, the visual appearance of products is a critical determinant of consumer response and product success (Crilly, Moultrie, & Clarkson, 2004). Applying this concept here, students are consumers of your course, and they make many judgments about your course product—its content, organization, relevance, and value—on the basis of the visual design of the syllabus. It is relatively easy to insert graphic elements in your syllabus, such as photos of the course content, images of students involved in learning experiences, or colorful tables, graphs, or pie charts. The language and visual design of your syllabus can have a positive impact on how your course is perceived by students and motivate them to follow you along the learning pathway.

Step 2: Write a Description of How Students Will Be Different

Make sure to include your dream for students and their learning in your syllabus, but you may need to help students see how accomplishing the course learning goals will lead to this dream.

When students read your syllabus, they want to know where you are taking them, what new capabilities they will have as a result of their work, what success looks like—what's in it for them, so to speak. This characteristic communicates that your course focuses on them and their learning successes. It sends the message that *their* learning success is *your* success—that you are in this together.

Revealing the goals shows students the end point, or destination, of the learning pathway. Recall from Chapter 4 that the power of goals to motivate learning lies in their clarity and transparency to students; their power is directly related to how students envision themselves accomplishing the goals on the summative assessment. Bain (2004) calls this "the promising syllabus" (pp. 74–75) because it explains the goals of the course in terms of a promise and begins a conversation about how the teacher and student can best come to understand the nature and progress of the student's learning. The promise of an aligned, transparent, and integrated course reassures students because they can see what the final exam, project, or paper begins to look like from the first day of the course. You can assure them that this is where the course is heading, and all activities are intentionally designed to help them accomplish the goals, which is another way you communicate the learning partnership. This is one reason we spend several hours developing goals during our course design retreat. However, simply placing goals in a syllabus without discussing how they function in your design relegates them to administrative, or irrelevant, information for students.

Step 3: Describe How Students Will Progress

Students are much more motivated to work and are likely to remain engaged if they know from your syllabus that your course takes them along the path to goals they personally value (Meece, Anderman, & Anderman, 2006). Students want to succeed on the summative assessment and demonstrate that they have accomplished the learning goals. Once they understand *where* they are going and the challenges ahead, they are interested in *how* they will get there. This is where the alignment and integration of your design stands front and center; students need to see that the the pathway leads to the goals and to success on the summative assessment. What projects, papers, or exams will be involved? How do they prepare for class? What will happen during a typical class session? An effective syllabus shows students the learning pathway that you develop through the design work in this book. The pathway includes the proficiencies they will need to achieve, the learning experiences that support them, and formative assessments that inform their progress. It is important to communicate this relationship between these elements, but it is not necessary to list all the proficiencies and learning experiences from your poster. Students simply need to see a sample of what's in store for them. This tells students why they are doing the work required in the course.

The learning challenges may be very intimidating to students, and it is important for your syllabus to show students how they will be supported in their learning. According to the challenge and support model, for growth to occur a person needs a balanced amount of challenge and support appropriate for the task (Sanford, 1966). Figure 10.1 shows the impact on students when the challenge matches or mismatches the level of support they receive. In Chapter 4 we advocate course goals that provide a high challenge that is developmentally appropriate, which in turn requires high levels of support that result in high performance and cognitive growth.

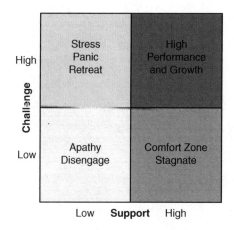

FIGURE 10.1. Students' Reactions to Different Levels of Challenge and Support

Based on *Self and Society: Social Change and Individual Development*, by N. Sanford, 1966, New York, NY: Atherton.

Support for learning is connected to the learning experiences, or what students will do during class and in their assignments outside class. This is how they encounter and experience the course. We propose a syllabus that outlines and describes a typical class session in which students practice thinking about and building their proficiencies (Paul & Elder, 2003). Is there a rhythm to a lesson? What level of participation will you ask of the students? Be sure students know that formative assessment and feedback will be part of their classroom experience; this sends the message that you value their learning progress and sets the rationale for student preparation and reinforcement. Next, we suggest describing how students prepare for in-class activities. What kinds of assignments and projects will you require? It is important to keep in mind the following: Be sure to frame the course work in a positive way (i.e., learning experiences support success), and only provide enough detail in the syllabus to give students a sense of what to expect. They don't need to know all the complex details at this point in time; complexity will only dilute and weaken your message.

Finally, students like a certain level of predictability, they want to know what to expect. If your course has a particular rhythm, such as lecture followed by student-led discussion followed by a quiz, then include this as part of their map along the learning pathway.

Use Workbox 10.2 to speak directly to the students, describing your pathway, your approach, or your strategy for guiding them to accomplish the course goals. Once again, this sends the message that the teaching-learning process is a partnership, an interaction that involves the appropriate levels of challenge and support.

Step 4: Add Administrative Information

In addition to being course designers, instructors are also course managers, so this part of the syllabus concerns your management of the course. Here you set expectations and boundary conditions, show students how you will observe their learning, and direct them to the available resources. In the following textbox, we list many common items in course syllabi that fall under course management. An abundant amount of advice available from books (e.g., Grunert O'Brien,

WORKBOX 10.2.
The Pathway to Achieve the Course Goals

Briefly describe how students will progress along the pathway to meet the goals of the course. Remember that your syllabus is speaking directly to the students:

Example: We have challenging goals this semester, let me briefly describe how the course is designed to support you to progress along the learning pathway to meet them.

Millis, & Cohen, 2008; Svinicki & McKeachie, 2013) and on websites elaborates on these items and may help you decide which administrative information you want to include. Go to https://styluspub.presswarehouse .com/products/buildingapathway.aspx to download a template that you can adapt to fit your specific context. While this template is rather straightforward in its approach, there are a few pitfalls to avoid.

Common Administrative Information in Syllabi

Course Information—public information

- Course title and description from catalog
- Prerequisites—informs students about their expected readiness for the course

Instructor Information—establishes lines of communication, credibility, and personal connections

- Contact information—office location, e-mail, telephone
- Office hours

Resources and References—support learning

- Books and textbooks—telling students why you selected them is always appreciated
- Electronic resources—online systems such as Blackboard, D2L, Moodle, and so on
- Course materials—study guides, problem solution guides, workbooks
- Support centers—writing center, student success center, math center

Grades and Grading—informs students of the workload and how their grade will be determined

- Graded events—papers, research projects, design projects, exams, quizzes, assignments
- Grades—criteria for student success

Policies and Expectations of Students—establishes boundaries

- Make sure all the necessary components of a course syllabus required by your institution are included.

WORKBOX 10.3.
Administrative Information

List the administrative information you want to include in your syllabus, and state how it functions in your course.

My syllabus includes the following:

In Workbox 10.3, write down the types of administrative information and policies you want to include in your syllabus.

Pitfall 1: Going Overboard Regarding Student Conduct

While many of these items are essential components of a syllabus, a few pitfalls regarding administrative information, especially in the areas of policies and expectations, should be avoided. Some instructors go overboard by trying to stop all potential forms of student irresponsibility or misconduct through their syllabus, which creates a negative tone and risks starting the semester off in a dictatorial manner. We suggest framing your conduct expectations in a positive way.

Pitfall 2: Giving Students More Information Than They Need

In many courses, syllabi are huge documents and faculty give students quiz credit just for reading them. We acknowledge that on some campuses, the syllabus is considered a contractual arrangement between the instructor and the student. Unfortunately, this places a large emphasis on policies and administrative information. Even when the syllabus has the role of a contract, you can avoid providing students with too much information at the start of the course by waiting until a later time when students are more receptive and inquisitive. For example, students probably don't need to know how the exams are formatted until a few lessons before the first exam. Too much information inevitably leads to a long administrative section in your syllabus, which drives two behaviors: either students don't read it, or you cover all of it on the first day of class to be sure they read it. Using class time in this way causes you to forfeit other opportunities to move forward and start meeting learning goals. You want the focus to be on student learning. At a minimum, students need to know what they should do for the second class meeting (e.g., buy books, register for the online component, complete a reading assignment, etc.).

Step 5: Examine the Template on the Website

Once you have downloaded the starting template for your syllabus from https://styluspub.presswarehouse .com/products/buildingapathway.aspx, we suggest you open it and begin filling in your syllabus, using the content of the workboxes in this chapter. Then, answer the following questions:

- Have you considered handing out the schedule or necessary policies and rules (e.g., compliance with disability laws and academic integrity policies) in separate documents?
- Is your syllabus designed to be a living document? For instance, is it flexible in case the information about student learning in your class causes you to slow down or speed up?
- After students read your syllabus will they understand your course and its design?

We invite you to use the starting template to begin the work of fleshing out and completing a syllabus that will effectively communicate your course design to students.

Conclusion

This chapter has guided you through four communication characteristics to help you make the decisions necessary to convert your course design into an effective syllabus. In effect, the syllabus begins to put your design into action, which now interacts with the student factors you considered in Chapter 3. Will your syllabus meet these four characteristics? Will it provide important information and transmit positive attitudes about your course? Will students understand your map and your vision for the course? Through your syllabus, you show students the pathway you have so carefully designed for their learning. In doing this you have begun to establish an environment conducive to learning for all students.

Designing college courses requires courage and openness to change, deep thinking, insights, and a high level of commitment to students. Implementing your design will bring many rewards and challenges with students, colleagues, and administrators. In the next and final chapter of the book, we use our experience in guiding others through this process to help answer questions and provide some advice on overcoming some potential challenges.

CHAPTER 11

Anticipating the Challenges Ahead

As we noted in Chapter 1, we and the higher education community at large (Barr & Tagg, 1995; Huba & Freed, 2000; Jones et al., 2009; Tagg, 2003) have learned a great deal in the past 20 years or so about what it means to be an effective college-level instructor. Ultimately, our measure of teaching success is tied to the quality of what our students learn. If they learn and develop in meaningful ways, we are successful. If they don't, we are not. It is that simple.

Despite the seeming simplicity of the learning-centered approach, faculty members don't spontaneously take that approach on their own when they design their courses. It doesn't always jibe with how things are normally done in their disciplines, among their faculty colleagues, or in their institution. Changing one's habits to take this approach often requires emotional shifts (i.e., giving up on old beliefs) as well as pedagogical shifts (i.e., new teaching skills). Doing things differently also requires courage and a sizable commitment to improving student learning. After working your way through the entirety of our course design process, we sincerely hope that the work you have done has a transformational effect on you, your course, and ultimately, your students.

One of the things you have certainly noticed about our approach to course design is that it works best when it is iterative and interactive. No one succeeds in creating a great course the first time, and we have consistently found that faculty members' thinking is improved by interacting with peers in and outside their discipline. The same can be said for the approach we have used at our course design retreat. Over the years we have learned a great deal about what works and what doesn't, and we are grateful to the dozens of faculty colleagues

who have worked with us through previous iterations of the retreat. Their hard work and thoughtful feedback have led to the process presented in this book.

At the end of our retreat, we reserve about an hour for a sort of town hall meeting with all the faculty members in attendance to ensure that they know the importance of their new social network as they begin to implement their course designs. Designing a course is hard work, but it can also be difficult for faculty colleagues to implement that new design once their semester begins. We and their fellow participants can provide an important support system as they encounter challenges moving forward. Similarly, we encourage you to draw upon the social support of your peers as you proceed with your work.

We also use the meeting to answer questions and anticipate potential challenges faculty members may face once back on campus. From year to year, the kinds of issues we discuss remain remarkably similar, and some questions are so common we thought we ought to address them in this closing chapter.[1] The following 15 questions, and our best attempts to answer each one, are divided into five categories: commitment to student learning, achieving buy-in from others, when students succeed and when they don't, implementing your course design, and the course design process and its applicability at other levels of student learning.

Category 1: Commitment to Student Learning

Am I ready to commit myself to student learning? Or, put another way, the instruction-centered approach

is easier because you don't have to think outside your head. Taking a students' perspective involves uncertainty and risk. Isn't it easier to just teach the class and hope for the best?

One faculty member who has participated in our retreat repeatedly tells us that she believes our model of course design is a better way to teach students, but we need to tell people that it is much more work (see also Weimer, 2002). In our experience, it is indeed easier for us to provide students with content and give them tests to see if they can remember. Therefore, the question you need to answer is about your own commitment.

Learning-centered teaching is more time consuming and can be more difficult to adapt to than the instruction-centered paradigm. We have a close colleague who continues to make changes to her design after multiple semesters teaching the same course. She has selected different materials, omitted course content, and created new and different learning experiences. Her commitment to student learning drives her continued reflection on the pathway of the course design she has built. She will be the first to say that it has been hard work and has required risk and flexibility. She would also be the first to say that the journey has been worth it.

My workload is already very high. How can I sustain my commitment to student learning in times when I am already stretched thin?

We know faculty are already working hard, particularly in an era of fewer colleagues, more institutional service, more student advising, greater scholarship demands, and so forth. However, as we reflect on works such as *Academically Adrift* (Arum & Roksa, 2011) and *We're Losing Our Minds* (Keeling & Hersh, 2011), we know it is time to do things differently. We need to make sure all our teaching behaviors—creating learning goals and summative assessments, brainstorming learning proficiencies, designing and implementing learning experiences, and formative assessment and feedback—are aligned with our students' learning.

Because sustaining the effort needed to commit to student learning can be difficult, we encourage you to draw on the strengths of like-minded colleagues, including peers you collaborate with in working through this book. A solid social network can give you encouragement when things get tough, and it can also

help you solve your teaching-related problems if or when you encounter them. If you are currently lacking a social network on your own campus, we encourage you to make contact with colleagues in your local teaching and learning center or professional organizations (such as the Professional and Organizational Development Network in Higher Education) dedicated to teaching excellence. You may contact us at buildinglearningpathways@googlegroups.com.

Category 2: Achieving Buy-In From Others

I am team teaching. How do I get my colleagues on board?

When colleagues ask you about the design of the course they are teaching with you, be aware that they probably have not given the same level of thought to the course that you have. Therefore, it is important for you to help them understand the process you used in thinking about your course. Start with an overview: your assumptions about student learning factors and the goals you have for student learning. If they accept this, then the rest of the course elements are likely to fall into place. Your course poster can serve as a guide in presenting additional details. Be patient, however. It will likely take you and your colleagues some time to reach a shared understanding about the pathway you are creating for student learning.

How do I get my students on board?

We have found that the vast majority of our students sincerely want to be successful and respond quite favorably to course designs that make what they need to do to succeed clear to them. That is why we think it is so important to develop a clear pathway students can follow to achieve the goals of your course. Once students begin to experience success along the pathway you have created, their interest in continuing will generally increase.

How do I get administrators' (e.g., supervisor, department head, dean) acceptance?

All courses contribute to the curriculum of a department, program, or institution. As a result, it is important to ensure that your course aligns with the expectations of these larger bodies. If you are asked about the details of your course, be prepared to describe the process you've gone through and your commitment to student learning. (Your poster can be useful in guiding these discussions.) You are designing a course that is totally transparent, aligned, and integrated so that your students have the best possible chance to meet the larger curricular outcomes, which means successful graduates and alumni.

While this may work at the Air Force Academy, how will it work at my institution, which is very different?

Every institution is distinctive in its own way—different students, different missions, and so on. However, one of the missions of all institutions of higher education is promoting student learning. Therefore, a course design process based on evidence of how people learn transcends any particular institutional setting. By working through the processes in this book, you can be successful no matter where you are teaching. We have seen this process work at institutions other than the Air Force Academy, and in our experience it is every bit as useful and effective in all contexts.

Category 3: When Students Succeed and When They Don't

If I focus on student learning, more of my students are likely to succeed. Does this mean that my expectations are too low and that I should be concerned?

You are correct that student success is likely to increase if you apply the course design process outlined in this book. Well-articulated goals give students a clear image of what they are trying to accomplish. Transparent, well-aligned course elements ensure that students focus their time and energy doing the kinds of things you want them to do. Meanwhile, the emphasis on engaging learning experiences, frequent assessment, and meaningful feedback provides students with the support they need to be successful.

None of this should suggest that your expectations are too low. In fact, we urge you to establish and uphold high expectations beginning with the learning goals from Chapter 4. A characteristic of effective goals is that they are appropriately challenging for the students in your course. Once established, those goals serve as

the foundation for all the other course design elements. If you have doubts about what you expect of students, revisit those goals and make sure they truly articulate the kind of learning you are after. If so, it is appropriate for you to provide students with the support they need to succeed in achieving the desired level of learning.

But what do I do if the average grades in my class go up?

By itself, an increase in students' grades is not a reason for concern; in fact it may be a cause for celebration. However, we understand that you may hear outcries about grade inflation from colleagues, departmental leadership, or the administration.[2] We encourage you to talk with those who are raising concerns; show them your course goals, your assignments, and the standards you used to evaluate student success. If you do so, it should be relatively easy to convince them that your course does indeed challenge students appropriately.

A powerful strategy is to maintain a portfolio of your students' work, which is especially helpful if you keep artifacts that span the entire range of student performance. Be sure to keep examples of some of your students' best work, but also keep examples of work that is not quite as strong. That way, your portfolio can show how the grades you assign in your course correspond to the work students actually do. Offering to review this portfolio with your colleagues or supervisors will almost certainly alleviate their concerns.[3]

Finally, if you find your students are consistently succeeding in meeting your learning goals, you might consider revising those goals to make them more rigorous. Perhaps your students are capable of handling even bigger challenges, and if that is the case, there is nothing wrong with pushing them to a higher level. The key is to modify the rest of your course design as well to ensure that you are offering students the support they need to meet those more ambitious goals.

What if my students don't succeed? In particular, what do I do if some of my students fall behind and have trouble catching up?

While our approach to course design places a clear emphasis on student learning success, there are obviously no guarantees that such learning will take place. If you encounter students who are having difficulty, we suggest that you first try to figure out the source or sources of the problem. Choosing an appropriate corrective action will depend on what is causing the shortcoming in the first place. For instance, you might consider any of the following:

- Have you missed any important student learning factors? That is, is there something about the students who are struggling that you didn't anticipate at the beginning stages of your course design? If so, how might you adjust other aspects of your course design to accommodate any unexpected needs?
- Have you chosen learning goals that are realistic for the students in your course? Sometimes, we find that faculty members set goals that are unattainable for the students enrolled in their courses. In those circumstances, faculty and students experience failure and frustration that could easily be avoided if only more realistic goals were chosen.
- Have you done a thorough job of outlining the proficiencies—knowledge, skills, and attitudes—needed to accomplish your learning goals (see Chapter 6)? If you have overlooked any of those proficiencies in constructing your course, it shouldn't be surprising to encounter students who have trouble succeeding.
- Are your learning experiences sufficient to help your students acquire the desired proficiencies? In some cases, providing additional learning experiences, inside or outside class, may be necessary to assist students who are struggling.
- Finally, are you offering adequate support for your students in the form of frequent formative assessment opportunities and meaningful feedback?

What if I double-check all the elements of my course, but there are still students who do poorly? Aren't the students ultimately responsible for their success as well?

Absolutely. This style of course design *requires* students to do their work, and if you've chosen appropriately challenging learning goals, the students will need to work hard to succeed. We want to ensure that students have the opportunity to be successful if they follow the path you've set out for them.

If you encounter students who are reluctant to follow the pathway you created for them, consider spending some time explaining how the pieces of your course fit together. The formative assessment element is especially important, as this is their time to practice and receive feedback on their success. That may be how we usually incorporate tests and quizzes and homework assignments, but students have a tendency to view their work on the basis of the grades they received or relative value in a course, not necessarily the value of the work as preparation for other elements of the course. Showing acquisition of a proficiency, whether it be a knowledge, skill, or attitude, puts them directly in a position to succeed. If you designed your course's learning experiences and formative assessments to develop students' proficiencies with increasing complexity, the elements are linked in such a way that students will need what has come earlier in the course. While this may be different from some of their previous experiences, be upfront with them about how to approach the work and why it is beneficial for them to do so.

Category 4: Implementing Your Course Design

In light of all the intentional planning of goals and assessments, are you advocating that faculty teach to the test?

The course design process we are advocating is based on the idea that a course's learning goals, proficiencies, learning experiences, and assessments should all be carefully aligned. If this is done well, it is understandable that one would think that you'd end up teaching to the test. However, this is not a bad thing. If teaching to the test means helping students learn the knowledge, skills, and attitudes needed to accomplish your course goals and then creating tests that measure the accomplishment of those goals, we argue that faculty *should* be teaching to the test. As Walvoord and Anderson (1998) say, "Why would we test and grade students on skills and subject matter we haven't taught them?" (p. 47).

Taken to the extreme, of course, teaching to the test could potentially be misconstrued as teaching the test, and we suspect this is what leads to this question. Teaching *to* the test strikes us as wholly appropriate;

we want faculty to structure their classes so that their learning experiences and assessments are aligned with the learning goals of the course. Teaching the test implies that faculty are training students how to answer particular questions on upcoming exams, which is very different and obviously poor practice. Teaching the test drives superficial pattern matching on the part of the student, whereas teaching *to* the test helps students develop deep connective strategies.

The course design I have come up with is a rather dramatic departure from what I have done in the past. Is there a way I can ease into my new course design so that I only change one course component this term and then change other components in the future?

Changing only one component of your course at a time is generally not a good idea because our course design model is based on creating an aligned, integrated system. Changing any one component (e.g., your learning goals) will lead to changes in other aspects of your course design (e.g., your assessments or learning experiences). Ironically, if you change one piece of the system but leave everything else the same, you are likely to end up making your course worse, simply because it will make the course poorly aligned.

Admittedly, changing multiple aspects of your course all at once can be a difficult thing to do. By now, however, we hope you are convinced it is the right thing to do. We ask that you trust your hard work and commit to using the course design you have created.

You've sold me on the need to teach my class in a way that focuses on student learning. Is there one specific teaching technique I can use in class that is best?

As appealing as a silver bullet would be, we're afraid that no such thing exists. As you've seen throughout this book, the learning experiences we provide for our students are part of a larger system that includes multiple course elements. As a faculty member, your challenge is to teach your class in a way that is well aligned and has the potential to get your students to accomplish what you want and need them to. A teaching technique that works very well in accomplishing one goal (and with one set of students) may not work very well in accomplishing a different goal (or with

a different set of students). On the other hand, multiple teaching techniques exist that would work well in a given circumstance. Therefore, the answer to the question of what teaching technique works best is: *it depends*.

In large part, that is why we favor a faculty development approach that emphasizes the thought processes associated with course design more than approaches that emphasize any specific teaching technique. It is impossible to say if any given technique is effective or not effective. The effectiveness of a technique is dependent on who your students are and what you are trying to accomplish. Only by considering the richer context of our overall course design can we begin to make informed decisions about the most appropriate ways to conduct our classes.

Category 5: The Course Design Process and Its Applicability at Other Levels of Student Learning

I get how I design my course with this model, but what do I do in each individual lesson?

The course design process in this book is powerful because the same process can be used at all levels of student learning. During each lesson, you recognize where your students are (student learning factors), identify the proficiencies you want students to obtain (often called objectives), plan out learning experiences to help students toward the proficiencies, and figure out the extent to which students are successful (assessment).

Is this approach also relevant when designing departmental or institutional curricula?

In short, yes. The same processes you have used to design your individual course can also be used to design entire curricula. The first step is to identify who your students are and how their entering characteristics will affect their learning. Then, articulate departmental or institutional learning outcomes, the final destination of your curricular pathway. Follow-up steps include aligned summative assessment tools, learning experiences, and formative assessment. This final step is especially important when considering curricular matters because it could help you identify the kinds of professional development faculty and staff need to create to achieve the kind of student learning administrators of the institution desire.

Concluding Thought

The list of questions in this chapter is based on those that we encounter most frequently, but it is certainly not exhaustive. If you have other questions, we invite you to contact us via our website at https://styluspub .presswarehouse.com/products/buildingapathway .aspx, where we will post questions we receive as well as our responses.

Notes

1. Although the questions in this chapter are based largely on our own experience, the same issues have been addressed in the larger higher education community as well. For a discussion of many of these issues, see Weimer (2002).

2. Rising grades by themselves are not sufficient evidence of grade inflation. One would need to show that students' grades are rising even though the overall quality of their work is not changing. If students' work is actually getting better, the grades associated with that work should reflect that improvement.

3. An added benefit of such a portfolio is that it can be used to show samples of student work to future cohorts of students in the same course, which would illustrate for them the pathway to success.

Appendix A

Rubric for Evaluating Course Posters

Course Designer/Course: _____

Reviewer: _____

Instructions: The quality of your course design will depend on the quality of your work with each element (i.e., student factors, learning goals, etc.), as well as how well those elements work together in your course. Each of these dimensions of quality is described in a lightly shaded row in the following rubric. To use the rubric, circle the one column (i.e., "exceptional," "good," or "needs work") in each row that most closely describes your judgment of that area. In addition, please use the white space in each row to add comments or suggestions for improvement.

	Exceptional—No improvements needed	Good—Only minor improvements needed	Needs Work—Major improvements needed
STUDENT LEARNING FACTORS	The student learning factors you have identified are likely to have a **high impact** on learning. The factors that have the greatest potential to affect learning success in the course are identified and accurately described.	The student learning factors you have identified are likely to have a **moderate impact** on student learning. Be mindful of other factors that could have a greater impact on achieving the learning goals.	The student learning factors you have identified are **not likely** to have a significant impact on student learning. There are almost certainly other factors that will have a greater impact on the success of your students.
Student learning factors are distinctive characteristics of your students that will affect how they will learn. (Refer to Chapter 3 for information about generating student learning factors.)	Use this space to write any comments/questions you have:		

	Exceptional—No improvements needed	Good—Only minor improvements needed	Needs Work—Major improvements needed
LEARNING GOALS	The stated learning goal is written in a way that is *entirely consistent* with the characteristics of effective goals: 1. Is clear and understandable to all 2. Focuses on student performance 3. Requires a high level of thinking that is developmentally appropriate 4. Connects components of the course 5. Is worthwhile and significant	The stated learning goal is written in a way that is *mostly consistent* with the characteristics of effective goals.	The stated learning goal is written in a way that is *substantially inconsistent* with the characteristics of effective goals.
Learning goals are what you want your students to know, feel, or be able to do as a result of taking your course. (Refer to Chapter 4 for information on constructing well-written learning goals.)	Use this space to write any comments/questions you have:		

	Exceptional—No improvements needed	Good—Only minor improvements needed	Needs Work—Major improvements needed
SUMMATIVE ASSESSMENT	The summative assessment is **well aligned** with the learning goal.	The summative assessment is **partially aligned** with the learning goal.	The summative assessment is **poorly aligned** with the learning goal.
Summative assessment is the tool or set of tools you will use to determine whether your students have achieved your learning goals by the end of the course. This will often take the form of a final exam, project, or presentation. (Refer to Chapter 5 for information about constructing an effective summative assessment.)	Use this space to write any comments/questions you have:		

	Exceptional—No improvements needed	Good—Only minor improvements needed	Needs Work—Major improvements needed
PROFICIENCES	You have identified the *most important proficiencies* necessary for students to accomplish the learning goal. Your poster reflects the most important knowledge, skills, and attitudes students will need to learn in your course.	You have identified *some of the most important proficiencies* necessary for students to accomplish the learning goal. You may wish to look at your list again to ensure that you include the most important proficiencies on your poster.	You have *left out the most important proficiencies necessary* for students to accomplish the learning goal. Please look at your list again to ensure that you include the most important proficiencies on your poster.
Proficiencies are the specific knowledge, skills, and attitudes your students need to accomplish your learning goals (and therefore to succeed on the summative assessment of the goals). (Refer to Chapter 6 for information on generating a good list of proficiencies.)	Use this space to write any comments/questions you have:		

	Exceptional—No improvements needed	Good—Only minor improvements needed	Needs Work—Major improvements needed
LEARNING EXPERIENCES	Learning experiences are *very likely to be sufficient* in helping students develop the learning proficiencies. The approach taken is highly effective.	Learning experiences are *probably sufficient* to help students develop the learning proficiencies. Perhaps they could be supplemented by more or better experiences.	Learning experiences are *likely to be insufficient* to help students develop the learning proficiencies. Significant changes are likely to be needed.
Learning experiences are any experiences students have that help them learn the desired proficiencies, including in-class experiences and out-of-class experiences. (Refer to Chapter 7 for information on choosing effective learning experiences.)	Use this space to write any comments/questions you have:		

	Exceptional—No improvements needed	Good—Only minor improvements needed	Needs Work—Major improvements needed
FORMATIVE ASSESSMENT	Formative assessment provides you and your students with *meaningful information* about students' acquisition of learning proficiencies, including information about what you or they need to do to improve.	Formative assessment provides you and your students with *some information* about students' acquisition of learning proficiencies. However, data are incomplete and may not provide sufficient information about what you and they need to do to improve.	Formative assessments are either missing or provide *inadequate information* about students' acquisition of learning proficiencies.
Formative assessment is the gathering of information about student learning in a way that can be used to improve the quality of that learning. This is the assessment performed during the course rather than at the end. (Refer to Chapter 8 for information on incorporating formative assessment opportunities in your course.)	Use this space to write any comments/questions you have:		

	Exceptional—No improvements needed	Good—Only minor improvements needed	Needs Work—Major improvements needed
TRANSPARENCY	The course's design is **highly transparent**. The course structure can be understood with minimal additional explanation from the course designer.	The course's design is **somewhat transparent**. The course structure can be understood but only with clarification from the course designer.	The course's design is **opaque**. The course structure cannot be understood without a detailed explanation from the course designer.
A course design is transparent when it is clear to all participants, including faculty, and students.	Use this space to write any comments/questions you have:		
OVERALL ALIGNMENT	This is a well-aligned course. **All elements** of the course point you and your students in the same direction—toward the desired learning goal.	This is a partially aligned course. **Most elements** of the course point you and your students in the same direction—toward the desired learning goal.	This is a poorly aligned course. **Few elements** of the course point you and your students in the same direction—toward the desired learning goal.
A course design is aligned when all the course elements (summative assessment, proficiencies, learning experiences, and formative assessments) point students in the same direction—toward the desired learning goal.	Use this space to write any comments/questions you have:		

	Exceptional—No improvements needed	Good—Only minor improvements needed	Needs Work—Major improvements needed
OVERALL INTEGRATION	This is a ***well-integrated*** course. There are areas of clear overlap between the summative assessment, proficiencies, learning experiences, and formative assessments associated with different course goals.	This is a ***partially integrated*** course. There may be areas of some overlap between the summative assessment, proficiencies, learning experiences, and formative assessments associated with different course goals, but they may seem somewhat artificial or forced.	This is a ***poorly integrated*** course. There is no apparent overlap between the summative assessment, proficiencies, learning experiences, and formative assessments associated with different course goals.
A course design is well integrated when the various goals of the course design work together to form a coherent whole. In other words, there are areas of clear overlap between the summative assessment, proficiencies, learning experiences, and formative assessments associated with different course goals.	Use this space to write any comments/questions you have:		

Appendix B

Taxonomy of the Psychomotor and Affective Domains

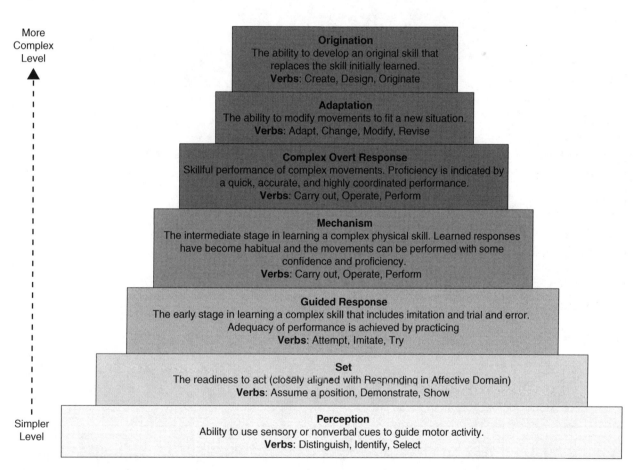

Adapted from *The Classification of Educational Objectives* in the *Psychomotor Domain: The Psychomotor Domain* (vol. 3), by E. J. Simpson, 1972, Washington, DC: Gryphon House.

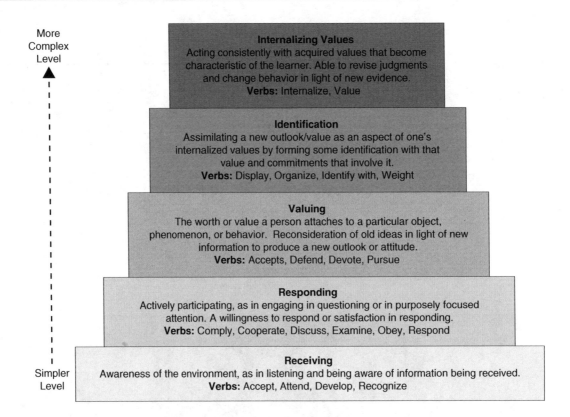

More
Complex
Level

▲
|
|
|
|
|
|
|
|
|
|
|
|
|
|
|
|
|
|
|

Simpler
Level

Internalizing Values
Acting consistently with acquired values that become
characteristic of the learner. Able to revise judgments
and change behavior in light of new evidence.
Verbs: Internalize, Value

Identification
Assimilating a new outlook/value as an aspect of one's
internalized values by forming some identification with that
value and commitments that involve it.
Verbs: Display, Organize, Identify with, Weight

Valuing
The worth or value a person attaches to a particular object,
phenomenon, or behavior. Reconsideration of old ideas in light of new
information to produce a new outlook or attitude.
Verbs: Accepts, Defend, Devote, Pursue

Responding
Actively participating, as in engaging in questioning or in purposely focused
attention. A willingness to respond or satisfaction in responding.
Verbs: Comply, Cooperate, Discuss, Examine, Obey, Respond

Receiving
Awareness of the environment, as in listening and being aware of information being received.
Verbs: Accept, Attend, Develop, Recognize

Adapted from *Taxonomy of Educational Objectives, Book II. Affective Domain*, by D. R. Krathwohl, B. S. Bloom, & B. B. Masia, 1964, New York, NY: David McKay.

Appendix C

Biology 320

Biomechanics

Spring 2012 Course Syllabus

Contact Information:

Guest Lecturers:

Text: *Basic Biomechanics, Sixth Edition* (2012), Susan J. Hall, McGraw Hill, San Francisco, CA. If any additional materials are used, they will be found on K:/DF/DFB/Bio 320

Course Description from Curriculum Handbook: Biology 320. Biomechanics. 3(1). A study of the physical, anatomical, mechanical, and physiological basis for motion focused on the human. Joint and muscle physiology will be explored as a basis for functional activities. Physics and mechanical engineering concepts will be applied to describe, investigate, and compare the ways we initiate and control movement. Students will also learn the effects musculoskeletal injury may have on normal motion. Final exam and/or final project. Prereq: Biology 210 or Biology 315; Engr Mech 220.

Course Goals: Following this course, students will be able to

Observe and describe a movement using the precise scientific language and principles of biomechanics.

This will include being able to

1. *Identify the functional anatomy (muscles)*
2. *Predict the forces acting on the joints and how they change during movement*
3. *Evaluate the performance of a movement on the basis of biomechanical factors (e.g., forces, velocities, and angles)*

Course Design: Biomechanics 320 is designed as a cyclical course. This means that you will be refining your understanding of human movement by doing similar assignments with increasing complexity as we move through a unit. We will add layers of new information as we progress. The core of all course assignments will be the papers describing the observation of human movements.

The Course Portfolio: In lieu of exams, each person is responsible for creating a course portfolio. This portfolio is meant to be a collection of ***and a reflection upon your work***. At the end, when you hand this in, it will be your responsibility to show me your learning. This should likely include evidence of where your understanding began and how it progressed. Scientific thinking will be required to succeed. At the core of scientific thinking, claims are based on evidence.

Your assignments and the items in your portfolio will constitute your evidence. We will talk in detail about this as we progress through the course. **NOTE: You are required to hand this in for a midterm grade on Lesson 20.**

Major Course Components:

  I. Introduction to Biomechanics
 II. Language of Biomechanics and Functional Anatomy
III. Physics of Movement—Forces
 IV. Maximizing Performance

Quizzes: I believe that learning is a growth process, and the papers and the portfolio will elicit your growth. That said, there is requisite information that is needed and to communicate your understanding of biomechanics and your observations of human movement. To ensure that you are keeping up with and developing an understanding of the principles and language of the field, and to give me feedback on how the class is accomplishing its goals, there will be **three scheduled quizzes** during the course. These will give both me and you an understanding of how well you are being prepared to complete your final paper and give us the tools to change things if needed. Quizzes will cover material presented in lecture, readings, or laboratory exercises and may consist of any combination of multiple choice, T/F, short answer, matching, and essay type questions.

Pop Quizzes: Quizzes and exams have the potential to elicit bulimic learning (binge and purge). Pop quizzes, on the other hand, allow me, as the instructor, insight into your held understanding. There will be **two pop quizzes** throughout the semester. One will be before prog; one after.

Papers: You will be responsible for **6 movement description and analysis papers** throughout the course. One will be the first paper, two will come in the course content areas of biomechanics language and functional anatomy; two in the course content area of physics and forces of movement; and finally, your concluding paper will include all of these plus a performance evaluation section. These papers will be graded on factual information describing your observation of human movement and on your ability to use feedback to improve. We should be able to read your paper in class and reconstruct the movements you observed from your writing. If you provide a perfect paper on the first try within a course content area, you can opt to validate the second paper in that unit. Rubrics will be made available for each paper when assigned. All documentation standards at USAFA apply.

Assignments: There will be **four homework assignments** during the semester.

Point Breakdown—note the weight of the portfolio (33%) and the papers (42%):

Graded Event	TENTATIVE Lesson #	Points
Quizzes—scheduled	9, 27, 32	75
Quizzes—pop	Unscheduled (1 before prog, one after)	50
HW assignments	Due on lesson 10, 14, 28, 33	125 (#1:50, all others 25)
Course portfolio midterm check	20	80
Course portfolio final	40	250
Papers (6)	3, 8, 15, 25, 29, 37	420 (#1:10, #2:50, #3:90, #4:50, #5:90, #6: 130)
Total	**Approx Points by Prog = 355 (35.5%)**	**Points in Course = 1000**

Course grades will be determined based on the following scale (*pending department head approval*):

93% or above = A	78–79% = C+
90–92% = A–	73–77% = C
88–89% = B+	70–72% = C–
83–87% = B	65–69% = D
80–82% = B–	<65% = F

References

Ahmad, J. (2012). *The teaching of biological sciences*. New Delhi, India: PHI Learning Private.

Åkerlind, G. S. (2007). Constraints on academics' potential for developing as a teacher. *Studies in Higher Education, 32*(1), 21–37.

Ambrose, S. A., Bridges, M. W., DiPietro, M., Lovett, M. C., & Norman, M. K. (2010). *How learning works: Seven research-based principles for smart teaching*. San Francisco, CA: Jossey-Bass.

American Psychological Association. (1997). *Learner-centered psychological principles: A framework for school reform & redesign*. Retrieved from at http://www.apa.org/ed/governance/bea/learner-centered.pdf

Anderson, J. R. (1982). Acquisition of cognitive skill. *Psychological Review, 89*(4), 369–406.

Anderson, L. W., & Krathwohl, D. R. (2001). *A taxonomy for learning, teaching, and assessing: A revision of Bloom's taxonomy of educational objectives*. New York, NY: Longman.

Angelo, T. A., and Cross, K. P. (1993). *Classroom assessment techniques: A handbook for college teachers* (2nd ed.). San Francisco, CA: Jossey-Bass.

Arum, R., & Roksa, J. (2011). *Academically adrift: Limited learning on college campuses*. Chicago, IL: University of Chicago Press.

Association of American Colleges and Universities. (2007). *College learning for the new global century*. Washington, DC: Author.

Astin, A. W. (1993). *What matters in college? Four critical years revisited*. San Francisco, CA: Jossey-Bass.

Bain, K. (2004). *What the best college teachers do*. Cambridge, MA: Harvard University Press.

Bandura, A. (1997). *Self-efficacy: The exercise of control*. New York, NY: Freeman.

Barkley, E. F. (2009). *Student engagement techniques: A handbook for college faculty*. San Francisco, CA: Jossey-Bass.

Barkley, E. F., Cross, K. P., & Major, C. H. (2005). *Collaborative learning techniques*. San Francisco, CA: Jossey-Bass.

Barr, R. B., & Tagg, J. (1995). From teaching to learning: A new paradigm for undergraduate education. *Change, 27*, 12–26.

Bassi, M., Steca, P., Delle Fave, A., & Vittorio Caprara, G. (2007). Academic self-efficacy beliefs and quality of experience in learning. *Journal of Youth and Adolescence, 36*, 301–312.

Biggs, J. (1996). Enhancing teaching through constructive alignment. *Higher Education, 32*, 347–364.

Biggs, J. (1999). What the student does: Teaching for enhanced learning. *Higher Education Research & Development, 18*(1), 57–75.

Black, P., & Wiliam, D. (1998). Assessment and classroom learning. *Assessment in Education, 5*(1), 7–74.

Bligh, D. A. (2000). *What's the use of lectures?* San Francisco, CA: Jossey-Bass.

Bloom, B. S. (1956). *Taxonomy of educational objectives, Handbook I: The cognitive domain*. New York, NY: David McKay.

Boice, R. (1998). Classroom incivilities. In K. A. Feldman and M. B. Paulson (Eds.), *Teaching and learning in the college classroom* (pp. 347–369). Needham Heights, MA: Simon & Schuster.

Bok, D. (2006). *Our underachieving colleges: A candid look at how much students learn and why they should be learning more*. Princeton, NJ: Princeton University Press.

Bok, D. (2013). *Higher education in America*. Princeton, NJ: Princeton University Press.

Bond, N. M. (1972). Effect of impression set on subsequent behavior. *Journal of Personality and Social Psychology, 24*(3), 301–305.

Bonwell, C. C. (1996). Enhancing the lecture: Revitalizing the traditional format. *New Directions for Teaching and Learning, 67*, 31–44.

Brookfield, S. (2005). *Discussion as a way of teaching*. San Francisco, CA: Jossey-Bass.

Campbell, J., & Smith, D. (1997, December). *Effective teaching for students with differing approaches to learning*. Paper presented at the meeting of the Australian Association for Research in Education, Brisbane.

Carey, K. (2011). "Trust us" won't cut it anymore. *Chronicle of Higher Education*. Retrieved from http://chronicle.com/article/Trust-Us-Wont-Cut-It/125978/

Carlson, K. A., & Winquist, J. R. (2011). Evaluating an active learning approach to teaching introductory statistics: A classroom workbook approach. *Journal of Statistics Education, 19*(1), 1–22.

Chickering, A., & Gamson, Z. F. (1987). Seven principles for good practice in undergraduate education. *American Association of Higher Education Bulletin, 39*(7), 3–7.

Cohen, S. A. (1987). Instructional alignment: Searching for a magic bullet. *Educational Researcher, 16*(8), 16–20.

College completion: Who graduates from college, who doesn't, and why it matters. (n.d). *Chronicle of Higher Education.* Retrieved from http://collegecompletion. chronicle.com

Crilly, N., Moultrie, J., & Clarkson, P. J. (2004). Seeing things: Consumer response to the visual domain in product design. *Design Studies, 25*(6), 547–577.

Davis, B. G. (2009). *Tools for teaching* (2nd ed.). San Francisco, CA: Jossey-Bass.

Deslauriers, L., Schelew, E., & Wieman, C. (2011). Improved learning in a large-enrollment physics class. *Science, 332*(6031), 862–864.

Diamond, R. M. (2008). *Designing and assessing courses and curricula: A practical guide* (3rd ed.). San Francisco, CA: Jossey-Bass.

Dobson, J. L. (2008). The use of formative online quizzes to enhance class preparation and success on summative exams. *Advances in Physiology Education, 32,* 397–302.

Duncan, D. (2005). *Clickers in the classroom: How to enhance science teaching using classroom response systems.* San Francisco, CA: Pearson Education.

Errington, E. R. (2003). *Developing scenario-based learning: Practical insights for tertiary educators.* Wellington, New Zealand: Dunmore Press.

Evans, C. (2013). Making sense of assessment feedback in higher education. *Review of Educational Research, 83*(1), 70–120. doi: 10.3102/0034654312474350

Fink, L. D. (2003). *Creating significant learning experiences: An integrated approach to designing college courses.* San Francisco, CA: Jossey-Bass.

Fink, L. D. (2005). *A self-directed guide to designing courses for significant learning.* Retrieved from http://www. designlearning.org/wp-content/uploads/2010/03/ Self-Directed-Guide..2.pdf

Freeman, S., Haak, D., & Wenderoth, M. P. (2011). *Increased course structure improves performance in introductory biology.* Retrieved from http://bit.ly/yYjGRc

Freire, P. (1998). *Pedagogy of freedom: Ethics, democracy, and civic courage.* Lanham, MD: Rowman & Littlefield.

Gardiner, L. F. (1998). Why we must change: The research evidence. *Thought & Action, 14*(1), 71–88.

Gardner, H. (1999). *Intelligence reframed.* New York, NY: Basic.

Gibbs, G., & Simpson, C. (2004). Conditions under which assessment supports students' learning. *Learning and Teaching in Higher Education, 1,* 3–31.

Grunert O'Brien, J., Millis, B., & Cohen, M. (2008). *The course syllabus: A learning-centered approach* (2nd ed.). New York, NY: Wiley.

Hake, R. R. (1998a). *Interactive-engagement methods in introductory mechanics courses.* Retrieved from at http://www.physics.indiana.edu/~sdi/IEM-2b.pdf

Hake, R. R. (1998b). Interactive-engagement vs. traditional methods: A six-thousand-student survey of mechanics test data for introductory physics courses. *American Journal of Physics, 66*(1), 164–174.

Hattie, J., & Timperley, H. (2007). The power of feedback. *Review of Educational Research, 77*(1), 81–112. doi: 10.3102/003465430298487

Heath, C., & Heath, D. (2007). *Made to stick: Why some ideas survive and others die.* New York, NY: Random House.

Huba, M. E., & Freed, J. E. (2000). *Learner-centered assessment on college campuses: Shifting the focus from teaching to learning.* Boston, MA: Allyn & Bacon.

Hubbard, D. W. (2011). *How to measure anything: Finding the value of intangibles in business.* Hoboken, NJ: Wiley.

Ishiyama, J., & Hartlaub, S. (2002). Does the wording of syllabi affect student course assessment in introductory political science classes? *PS: Political Science and Politics, 3,* 567–570.

Johnson, M. (2009). *Professor Dancealot.* Retrieved from http://www.youtube.com/watch?v=1k8aeDUC0XQ

Jones, S. K., Sagendorf, K., Morris, D., Stockburger, D., & Patterson, E. (2009). Lessons learned from developing a learning-focused classroom observation form. In L. Nilson & J. Miller (Eds.), *To improve the academy* (Vol. 27, pp. 199–222). San Francisco, CA: Jossey-Bass.

Keeling, R. P., & Hersh, R. H. (2011). *We're losing our minds: Rethinking American higher education.* New York, NY: Palgrave Macmillan.

Kember, D., & Gow, L. (1994). Orientations to teaching and their effect on the quality of student learning. *Journal of Higher Education, 65*(1), 58–74.

King, P. M., & Kitchener, K. S. (2004). Reflective judgment: Theory and research on the development of epistemic assumptions through adulthood. *Educational Psychologist, 39*(1), 5–18.

Kitchener, K. S., & King, P. M. (1981). Reflective judgment: Concepts of justification and their relationship to age and education. *Journal of Applied Developmental Psychology, 2*(2), 89–116.

Kohlan, R. G. (1973). A comparison of faculty evaluations early and late in the course. *Journal of Higher Education, 44*(8), 587–595.

Krathwohl, D. R., Bloom, B. S., & Masia, B. B. (1964). *Taxonomy of educational objectives, Book II. Affective domain.* New York, NY: David McKay.

Lumina Foundation for Education. (2011). _The degree qualifications profile_. Retrieved from http://www.lumina-foundation.org/publications/The_Degree_Qualifications_Profile.pdf

Marcus, N., Cooper, M., & Sweller, J. (1996). Understanding instructions. _Journal of Educational Psychology_, _88_(1), 49–63.

Mayer, R. (2003). _Learning and instruction._ Upper Saddle River, NJ: Merrill Prentice-Hall.

Mayer, R. E., (2001). _Multimedia learning._ Cambridge, UK: Cambridge University Press.

Meece, J. L., Anderman, E. M., & Anderman L. H. (2006). Classroom goal structure, student motivation, and academic achievement. _Annual Review of Psychology_, _57_, 487–503.

Millis, B. J. (2010). _Cooperative learning in higher education._ Sterling, VA: Stylus.

Morrison, G. R., Ross, S. M., & Kemp, J. E. (2001). _Designing effective instruction_ (3rd ed.). New York, NY: Wiley.

National Research Council. (2000). _How people learn: Brain, mind, experience, and school._ Washington, DC: National Academies Press.

Newton, L. (1990). _Overconfidence in the communication of intent: Heard and unheard melodies._ Unpublished doctoral dissertation, Department of Psychology, Stanford University.

Nilson, L. B. (2003). Improving student peer feedback. _College Teaching_, _51_(1), 34–38.

Nilson, L. B. (2007). _The graphic syllabus and the outcomes map: Communicating your course._ San Francisco, CA: Jossey-Bass.

Nilson, L. B. (2010). _Teaching at its best: A research-based resource for college instructors (3rd ed.)._ San Francisco, CA: Jossey-Bass.

Novak, G., & Patterson, E. (2010). An introduction to just-in-time teaching (JiTT). In S. Simkins and M. H. Maier (Eds.), _Just-in-Time Teaching_ (pp. 3–23). Sterling, VA: Stylus.

Noyd, R. K., & Staff of the Center for Educational Excellence. (2008). _A primer on writing effective learning centered course goals_ (White paper 08-01). Colorado Springs, CO: U.S. Air Force Academy.

Nuhfer, E., & Knipp, D. (2003). The knowledge survey: A tool for all reasons. _To Improve the Academy_, _21_, 59–78.

Palomba, C. A., & Banta, T. W. (1999). _Assessment essentials._ San Francisco, CA: Jossey-Bass.

Pascarella, E., & Terenzini, P. (1991). _How college affects students._ San Francisco, CA: Jossey-Bass.

Paul, R., & Elder, L. (2003). _A miniature guide on how to improve student learning._ Dillon Beach, CA: Foundation for Critical Thinking.

Pennebaker, J. W., Gosling, S. D., & Ferrell, J. D. (2013). Daily on-line testing in large classes: Boosting college performance while reducing achievement gaps. _PLoS ONE_, _8_(11): e79774. doi: 10.1371/journal.pone.0079774

Pintrich, P. R., & De Groot, E. V. (1990). Motivational and self-regulated learning components of classroom academic performance. _Journal of Educational Psychology_, _82_(1), 33–40.

Prince, M. (2004). Does active learning work? A review of the research. _Journal of Engineering Education_, _93_(3), 223–231.

Richlin, L. (2006). _Blueprint for learning: Creating college courses to facilitate, assess, and document learning._ Sterling, VA: Stylus.

Robinson, K. (2010a, May 24). _Bring on the learning revolution!_ [Video file]. Retrieved from http://www.youtube.com/watch?v=r9LelXa3U_I

Robinson, K. (2010b, October 14). _Changing education paradigms_ [Video file]. Retrieved from http://www.youtube.com/watch?v=zDZFcDGpL4U

Sanford, N. (1966). _Self and society: Social change and individual development._ New York, NY: Atherton.

Simpson, E. J. (1972). _The classification of educational objectives in the psychomotor domain: The psychomotor domain_ (Vol. 3). Washington, DC: Gryphon House.

Stevens, D. D., & Levi, A. J. (2012). _Introduction to rubrics: An assessment tool to save grading time, convey effective feedback, and promote student learning_ (2nd ed.). Sterling, VA: Stylus.

Summers, L. H. (2012). What you (really) need to know. _New York Times._ Retrieved from http://www.nytimes.com/2012/01/22/education/edlife/the-21st-century-education.html

Svinicki, M., & McKeachie, W. (2013). _McKeachie's teaching tips_ (14th ed.). San Francisco, CA: Cengage Learning.

Tagg, J. (2003). _The learning paradigm college._ Bolton, MA: Anker.

Tapscott, D. (2009, June 4). _The impending demise of the university._ Retrieved from http://edge.org/conversation/the-impending-demise-of-the-university

Thiel Foundation. (2011). _The Thiel Fellowship._ Retrieved from http://www.thielfellowship.org/become-a-fellow/about-the-program/

Thorndike, E. L. (1922). _The psychology of arithmetic._ New York, NY: Macmillan.

Treisman, U. (1992). Studying students studying calculus: A look at the lives of minority mathematics students in college. _The College Mathematics Journal_, _23_(5), 362–372.

Trigwell, K., & Prosser, M. (1996). Changing approaches to teaching: A relational perspective. _Studies in Higher Education_, _21_(3), 275–284.

U.S. Department of Education. (2006). *A test of leadership: Charting the future of U.S. higher education*. Retrieved from http://www2.ed.gov/about/bdscomm/list/hied-future/reports/pre-pub-report.pdf

VanLehn, K. (1996). Cognitive skill acquisition. *Annual Review of Psychology, 47*, 513–539.

Walvoord, B. E., & Anderson, V. J. (1998). *Effective grading: A tool for learning and assessment*. San Francisco, CA: Jossey-Bass.

Weimer, M. (2002). *Learner-centered teaching: Five key changes to practice*. San Francisco, CA: Jossey-Bass.

Wesch, M. (2007, October 12). *A vision of students today* [Video file]. Retrieved from http://www.youtube.com/watch?v=dGCJ46vyR9o

White, R., & Grunstone, R. (1992). *Probing understanding*. Philadelphia, PA: Falmer Press.

Wieman, C. (2007). Why not try a scientific approach to science education? *Change, 39*(5), 9–15.

Wiggins, G. P. (1993). *Assessing student performance: Exploring the purpose and limits of testing*. San Francisco, CA: Jossey-Bass.

Wiggins, G., & McTighe, J. (2005). *Understanding by design: Expanded second edition*. San Francisco, CA: Pearson Education.

Willingham, D. T. (2009). *Why don't students like school?* San Francisco, CA: Jossey-Bass.

Yair, G. (2000). Reforming motivation: How the structure of instruction affects students' learning experiences. *British Educational Research Journal, 26*(2), 191–210.

About the Authors

Robert K. Noyd, Kenneth S. Sagendorf, Steven K. Jones (Photo courtesy of Kris Jones.)

Steven K. Jones is an associate professor of behavioral sciences and leadership at the United States Air Force Academy (USAFA). He has taught for more than 20 years in university and service academy classrooms. For the past 10 years, he has served as the director of academic assessment in USAFA's Center for Educational Excellence. He works closely with faculty across the institution on matters of effective course design, particularly as it pertains to assessment of course learning goals and departmental/institutional learning outcomes. His scholarly contributions are focused on the clear articulation, development, and assessment of institutional learning outcomes.

Robert K. Noyd is professor of biology at the United States Air Force Academy where he teaches botany, general biology, and senior seminar courses. He has taught for more than 35 years in high school, community college, small college, university, and service academy classrooms. He has served as USAFA's director of faculty development and continues to write innovative

educational materials and present workshops throughout the country on course design and learning-focused strategies. His new, first-edition biology textbook uses research-based principles of learning to motivate and inspire students nationwide.

Kenneth S. Sagendorf is the founding director of the Center for Excellence in Teaching and Learning (CETL) and a professor at Regis University——a Jesuit University in Denver, CO. He holds degrees in biology (BS), applied exercise physiology (MS), and College Science Teaching (PhD). In more than 20 years in higher education, he has worked as a faculty member and administrator at four academic institutions—from small state schools to research institutions to the United States Air Force Academy. His own scholarship focuses on creating environments and cultures conducive to student learning—at the lesson, course, program, and curricular levels. His publications include books on incorporating disability into the college classroom and curriculum and promoting academic integrity through classroom instruction.

Index

Companion Website

As you will see, course design can be difficult work, and we have found that it is most effective when the process is both interactive and iterative. To support you in the process, we have created a free companion website that includes all the workboxes you will find in the text. The website not only enables you to complete each workbox but also displays a pathway for each course goal in the form of a poster. You can name and save each iteration or new design that you create to both the Cloud and your hard drive so you can retrieve your work at will or share it with colleagues.

As you complete the culminating workbox for each chapter, the text you enter will automatically fill in the relevant portion of your course poster. Where applicable, that text will also automatically fill in the corresponding column of a workbox in a subsequent chapter. This will save you time, and it will also reinforce the interrelated nature of the design process. For instance, identifying particular knowledge that students must have (in Chapter 6) leads you to identifying one or more appropriate learning experiences (in Chapter 7).

Website URL: https://styluspub.presswarehouse.com/products/buildingapathway.aspx

We also recommend using the website workboxes in connection with workshops and faculty learning communities. If you would like multiple copies of the book for use in such settings, Stylus Publishing offers discounts for quantity orders. For more information call 1-800-232-0233, or e-mail stylusmail@presswarehouse.com.

We are happy to work with you and your institutional colleagues as you develop courses that deepen and strengthen student learning.

We welcome you to contact us at buildinglearningpathways@googlegroups.com .

Steve, Bob, & Ken

Sty/us

22883 Quicksilver Drive
Sterling, VA 20166-2102

Subscribe to our e-mail alerts: www.Styluspub.com